SUSAN CRAIN BAKOS

Sexational Secrets

EROTIC ADVICE YOUR
MOTHER NEVER GAVE YOU

St. Martin's Press ❧ New York

FOR WESLEY, OUR PASHA,
JANE, THE ROYAL WIFE,
AND OUR HAREM SISTERS,
CAROLYN AND MARILYN

Book design by Gretchen Achilles

Library of Congress Cataloging-in-Publication Data

Bakos, Susan Crain.
    Sexational secrets : erotic advice your mother never gave you /
Susan Crain Bakos.— 1st ed.
        p.   cm.
    ISBN 0-312-14413-X
    1. Sex.   2. Sexual excitement.   3. Sex (Psychology)   I. Title.
HQ31.B235 1996
306.7—dc20   96-6009
                                                                CIP

First Edition: August 1996

10 9 8 7 6 5 4 3 2 1

Books are available in quantity for promotional or premium use. Write to Director of Special Sales, St. Martin's Press, 175 Fifth Avenue, New York, N.Y. 10010, for information on discounts and terms, or call toll-free (800) 221-7945. In New York, call (212) 674-5151 (ext. 645).

CONTENTS

Introduction: Why Not You?

Are some people having multiple orgasms, extended orgasms, nongenital orgasms, whole-body orgasms, electrifying oral experiences, incredible and emotionally intense lovemaking sessions that last for hours?

Unbelievable as it may sound—yes.

Why not you?

The best *gourmet* sex advice doesn't come from therapists who work primarily on relationships and the treatment of sexual dysfunctions, but from varied and exotic sources. American call girls, French courtesans, Japanese geishas, suave European gigolos, and kept women of the world. Sex gurus from Tibet and practitioners of Tantric and Taoist sex. People like Betty Dodson and Joe Kramer, who teach classes in masturbation, or Stephanie Wadel, the teacher of Cherokee sexuality, and Kuttra Decostered, founder of Kahua Hawaiian Institute, which instructs devotees in Ocean Tantra, a combination of Tantric and American Indian rituals and the language of dolphins. Or former porn stars and belly dancers who give classes on seduction or foreplay through the Learning Annex in New York and similar adult education facilities.

This kind of erotic advice is primarily available in big cities. You may be prohibited from attending by geography, financial or time constraints, or other factors, including reluctance to be sexual in a public setting. For example, some people who are financially able to take Annie Sprinkle's workshop on how to have a fire-breathing orgasm don't because they're too embarrassed to get down on the floor with fifty other women to try to breathe their way to ecstasy with Annie's enthusiastic help.

As a journalist who's spent a dozen years exclusively covering sex, I will take you inside the workshops, seminars, classes, and conferences—the kind you won't find listed in your local community college catalog or posted on the church bulletin board beside the marriage retreat notices. These are places where you can't or won't go yourself to get sizzling erotic advice from outrageous and fascinating people, the ultimate sex experts of our time. I have been there and done that and prepared a report, including clear instructions, for you to read in bed with your partner. You will not have to wade through a stack of esoteric Eastern sex books to get to the good parts or spend hundreds of dollars on seminars given by people who take themselves just a bit too seriously. This is sex, not brain surgery. Nor will you embarrass yourself in public trying to learn something while wearing street clothes that should be learned in the nude.

Like the *Kama Sutra,* that enduring sex advice book written many centuries ago, *Sexational Secrets* is graphic in the explanations of techniques and positions. May it bring pleasure to you and your partner. Enjoy!

Part 1

IT'S LARGELY IN THE BRAIN:
THINK, TALK, AND TEASE

Chapter One

BUILDING A LONG DESIRE

*L*isa was eloquent in describing her longing for Mac, her boyfriend of sixteen years, who spends weeks, sometimes months at a time, working as an engineering consultant on projects in the Far East. Frequent separations have helped to create a superheated relationship. Both foreign service officers at the time, they met six weeks before he was scheduled to leave the country for a three-year tour of duty in Morocco and the very day she'd received a promotion and been reassigned to Paris. They had four weeks in the same city before the leavetakings began.

The romance of their destinations alone was like a musky perfume in the air between them. Like lovers who meet during wartime, they were emboldened as much by the scarcity of their time together as by the strength of their passion. And, at the time, foreign service officers were discouraged from dating each other. Add another element to the erotic stew: the forbidden factor.

"We made love on the first date," she said. "I couldn't get enough of him that day. We spent most of those four weeks together every night—and it still wasn't enough.

"The last time we were together we only had twelve hours. I won't see him again for a month. When I know he's going away—

or I am—I can't get enough of him. I'm trying to fill myself up. I've never known the meaning of the word *yearn* before this man. With him, once is never enough."

How do people sustain the intense longing of a new love if one or the other of them isn't always dashing off to Morocco or similar exotic locales?

Memorable sexual experiences often fall into one of two categories: first times, either the first time you made love or performed fellatio with anyone, or the first time you experienced these things with a particular partner, or serendipitous encounters, where the partner, the setting, the unexpected opportunity for uninhibited pleasure—all the better if it is forbidden—are present at the same time.

How many firsts and serendipitous encounters will any of us have in our lives? Almost everyone wants a committed relationship, be it marriage or a regular date for Saturday night. We get tired of sharing dinners with strangers who are evaluating us as we are them. We worry about sexually transmitted diseases. And we long for the emotional warmth and safety found only with someone who knows and loves us. But we still want the excitement of the new. Is it possible to have both with the same person?

Sex can get boring in a committed relationship because you know there will be sex more or less when you want it and in the way you've had it before. Sex becomes predictable. Where is the mystery? When does the yearning have a chance to develop? How can two people who have been together awhile possibly rediscover the feelings generated by their first times?

Jack Morin, a California author, said in his book *The Erotic Mind* that the formula for hot sex is simply:

ATTRACTION + OBSTACLES = EXCITEMENT

You need to strew a few obstacles in your path to the bed. That may be why some couples fight so much. But there are other ways. The ancient Egyptians were as sentimental and romantic about love as modern Westerners. Their word for *love,* loosely translated, means "a long desire." Egyptian love poems—filled with the separations and calamities that keep lovers apart—and romantic fiction, from Shakespeare's *Romeo and Juliet* to Harlequin romances, have capitalized on the formula Attraction + Obstacles = Excitement to hold readers' attention and sometimes, as in the case of the Bard's tragic lovers, the world's imagination for centuries.

Typically the fictional couple must surmount obstacles, which may include geographical distance, the initial uninterest of one partner, or the social unsuitability of the match because of racial, cultural, or economic differences. They long for each other and eagerly anticipate the pleasure they will take in each other's bodies when the opportunity finally arrives. They exist in the state of *ragavat,* the passionate love of the *Kama Sutra,* born of intense physical attraction.

Why does the romance novel end when they get married? They will soon slide into the state of *Aharyaraga,* the love of habit and affection, the result of long cohabitation. And who wants to read about that?

Great sex—the sustaining of *ragavat*—requires a balance between intimacy and separateness. In America we overemphasize intimacy at the expense of separateness. "Let there be spaces in your togetherness," Kahlil Gibran said in *The Prophet.* Independence can be an aphrodisiac. Yet who isn't tempted to hold tightly, particularly when a lover's passion seems to be waning—just at the point where separate vacations might be a better idea?

Some couples believe that working on "the problem" of flagging desire will lead them back to the passion they once had. One of the common prescriptions from advice columnists and sex therapists for such a couple is the sex date, scheduled time for lovemaking. Can you work and schedule your way back to passion? Is this really the path to the long desire? There is a better way for building erotic hunger: *denial.*

Sophisticated lovers have learned that delaying orgasm can intensify the pleasure (and you will find many techniques for doing that in the chapters ahead). A skillful man or woman can tease his or her lovers to the edge of orgasm, stop and pull them back from ecstasy into delicious erotic torment, and tease them again—taking them from one plateau of arousal to a higher one, until they finally explode in orgasmic ecstasy. How high up the erotic mountain might they travel if the delaying took place after a period of denying?

During the Ming Dynasty in China, from the mid-fourteenth through sixteenth centuries, a bizarre practice, a form of sexual alchemy based on denial of pleasure, was popularized at court by Taoist priests. In the art of *tsai-pu,* or "pluck and nurture," each partner tried to "pluck" the orgasmic secretions of the other, believing that he or she was nurturing his or her own sexuality with the precious fluids. To pluck without being plucked—to cause your partner to have an orgasm while you held back your own climax—could improve your health, increase your life span, and enhance your sexuality, or so it was believed.

According to Valentin Chu, San Francisco authority on ancient Chinese sexology, this practice was a "perversion" of earlier Taoist teachings and also had another purpose beyond "rejuvenation." A man who had repeatedly absorbed female secretions without ejaculating would produce superior semen, which would enable him to father a superior son when he did finally ejaculate. *Tsai-pu* aficionados were the "the really rich and decadent middle-aged men who kept stables of pampered concubines to pluck."

We won't be taking denial that far.

𝒯HINK ABOUT IT, BUT DON'T DO IT . . . YET

Most couples practice occasional celibacy only when it's enforced by physical separation. Reunion sex is typically a four-star event for them. Why not have that event without the travel time?

A couple of thousand years ago the Chinese Taoists developed an erotic philosophy based on a few simple ideas, including denial as a means of building sexual appetite. They believed that good sex promoted health and longevity in both men and women. Their followers were admonished to live neither the celibate life nor follow the path of sexual excess. But the Taoists understood the role of occasionally holding back, both in creating desire by not making love every time they experienced arousal and in extending orgasms by delaying orgasm when they did make love. The men were encouraged to indulge in frequent loveplay without ejaculation. (For techniques, see page 201.) And both men and women were taught that occasionally not acting upon erotic feelings encouraged stronger feelings the next time.

As I discovered, the power of denial in creating desire is so strong that it can overcome the jet lag induced by a seventeen-hour flight from New York City to Bombay, India, a ten-and-a-half-hour time zone leap, and another two hours going through the process of claiming bags and passing customs. At the end of that journey my lover was waiting. We hadn't seen each other in two months. What would be stronger: desire or fatigue? *The power of the long desire.*

Making love in the car would have been an insult to our driver, but I began thinking about the lovemaking we were going to share while riding from the airport in a car passing male and female prostitutes and the eunuch beggars lining Juhu Beach Road, past the road leading toward Bollywood, India's Hollywood, and the homes of the wealthy and glamorous denizens of the film industry. As my lover gestured at buildings from the days of the Raj with towers and canopied balconies and ornate grillwork and the occasional gargoyle on high, I pictured him naked the last morning we'd spent together in my bed before he left for India. I saw him asleep, lying on his side, the smooth curve of muscled buttock and thigh, the small patch of hair at the base of his spine.

"Look at the elephant lumbering along the side of the road," he said, and I remembered lying behind him, waking, touching the patch of hair, and gently brushing my lips across that solid curve.

After we arrived at the Taj Mahal Hotel, I still needed some private minutes in the shower to coax those mental erotic buds into full bloom, so I didn't invite him to join me. Alone in the bathroom, I ignored the mothballs in the drain meant to discourage enormous bugs from crawling out of them and closed my eyes and saw his body on top of mine. He, holding fast to my hips.

I ran my own hands lovingly over my body. My fingers slick with soap, I made wet wide circles around my nipples. I caressed my belly, hips, and thighs, and gently pressed my hands against my vulva. Knowing his hands would soon replace mine excited me further. Dire burned away the fatigue.

When I'd packed for India, I included the black silk teddy that makes me feel more desirable than any other item of clothing I own. After my shower, I slipped into the teddy and the thigh-high lace-topped stockings he loves. As I came out of the bathroom, I saw that he had lit several fat candles. A bottle of champagne nestled in a bucket of ice by the bed. Although I didn't drink the champagne—it would have put me to sleep—just having it there made me feel glamorous.

Later, lying sated in my lover's arms, I drowsily watched the sky outside our hotel room window fill with the grayish pink light that heralds dawn on the subcontinent. The honey-colored basalt outlines of the Gateway to India, that picturesque landmark on the bay, loomed large as he lovingly stroked my face and I fell asleep.

How did I do it? More important, how do *you* do it? Let's begin with that truest of old clichés: Sex is largely between the ears.

$\mathscr{T}$HE PRE-SEX MINDSET

Actively fantasizing about a sexual encounter in graphic detail before it occurs is called "mental preimaging." This technique, which many easily orgasmic women use, made my first night in Bombay memorable. It can help you overcome fatigue, tension, and stress and put you in the mood for lovemaking.

Easily orgasmic women are defined by most researchers as those who are orgasmic in over 90 percent of their encounters with a partner. They share certain behavioral traits, which were first defined by

Marc and Judith Meshorer in their landmark study of easily orgasmic women, *Ultimate Pleasures.* Those traits include:

- STARTING ON WARM. Encourage those fleeting sexual thoughts that intrude into the workday. Take time to bathe and dress, including caressing your own body, before an anticipated sexual encounter. In effect, easily orgasmic women jumpstart their bodies rather than waiting for the man to initiate the erotic process.

- INDULGING IN EROTIC ENTERTAINMENT. Read erotica, seek out erotic films, including the X-rated variety, and appreciate erotic art from the sublime to the ads for Calvin Klein underwear.

- CONVEYING INTENTIONS. Have you ever called your man at the office to tell him you've taken off your panties and you're on your way home? That's "conveying intentions." It may sound like a Cosmo girl ploy, but the truth is: Cosmo girls are probably having better sex than most people are.

- MENTAL PREIMAGING. Use active erotic mental activity to prepare for lovemaking. This is deliberate down and dirty fantasizing, no cut from the chase allowed. Feel the strong physical sensations in your body. If you see his mouth on your clitoris, you *feel* his mouth on your clitoris.

I asked a group of eight easily orgasmic women who'd been part of a research study to indulge in this typical preparatory behavior, *but not have sex!*—and to do this for two or three days a week, if possible. The women ranged in age from twenty-eight to forty-four, five were married or living with a partner, three were not. They reported an increase in mental sexual activity, which led to an acute yearning to make love to their partners. The long desire.

One women said, "For a week, I practiced the arousal patterns without having sex—and did not allow myself the release of masturbation either. By the end of the week, my desire for my partner was more intense than it had been in years. I wanted everything all at once. I wanted him to caress every part of me while he was kissing me and entering me. And I wanted to touch and kiss and lick and suck. I couldn't get enough of him."

And from another: "I did this for ten days. I wouldn't have gone so long if my husband hadn't left on a business trip toward the end of my little experiment in denial. I was wild for him by the time he got back. The last day I was bombarded with unbidden sex fantasies. I was ready to explode. The orgasms were tremendous."

The combination of mental preimaging and practicing denial can create explosive sex. Think how great food tastes after you've fasted. Well, it's better than that.

THE ULTIMATE SEXUAL HEAD TRIP FOR WOMEN ONLY: THE SPONTANEOUS ORGASM

When I first heard about a workshop where women could learn to have spontaneous orgasms, I thought it sounded like a situational oxymoron. If something is spontaneous, how can you learn to do it? Then I imagined thousands of women who've been taught this secret crying out in ecstasy in the most unlikely places. Women who couldn't stop themselves from coming on line at the ATM, in editorial meetings, the dentist's chair. Women with bangs pasted to their foreheads, raccoon eyes from running mascara, damp clinging silk blouses—a heaving mass of orgasmic women bursting from their business suits, like a life-size *Penthouse* mural painted across public buildings.

I decided to attend the workshop. The other participants did not look ready to erupt in orgasm at any moment. Ranging in age from the twenties to perhaps the early sixties, they were similar in appearance to groups of women assembled for literary readings, lectures on art, or Chinese cooking classes. Some wore business suits with heels, while some wore business suits with socks and sneakers, their shoes in their roomy tote bags, the city woman's foot-survival tactic. A few were dressed in jeans or casual clothes. They all had the eager, open, and receptive faces of people who have come to learn something new or perfect the technique they were already using. While most of us had never tried to have a fire-breathing orgasm, seven women had.

"I have been trying to figure out how to do it from a book," said a college professor. "I'm not quite there."

"I know someone who says she does it," a department store buyer said. "I want to learn so that I can have an orgasm during sex without having to touch myself. My boyfriend will think he's done it for me at last."

Annie Sprinkle, former porn star and performance artist, the workshop leader, assured us that learning how to have a "fire-breathing," no-hands, no-touch orgasm wouldn't reprogram our bodies so that we might spontaneously combust in erotic meltdown at inopportune moments. No, this was a technique for having an orgasm whenever we wanted *without touch.*

"Why bother?" someone asked Annie. "I like to touch."

"Why not learn a new way of experiencing pleasure?" Annie countered, stressing the no-touch orgasm as an addition to, not a supplement for, touch orgasm.

We could, Annie promised, achieve a mind-blowing orgasm by getting our sensory neurons to fire on fantasy alone. Why not a brain-only orgasm?

Some women can have them, though the research literature offers paltry examples of "spontaneous orgasm," the clinical term for orgasm without touch. Kinsey reported only 2 percent of his sampling of women could reach orgasm by fantasy alone. Shere Hite found less than 1 percent. Masters and Johnson, whose work focused primarily on people with sexual dysfunctions, reported that none of their subjects experienced spontaneous orgasms. On the other hand, Marc and Judith Meshorer found several. And Gina Ogden, Ph.D., claimed that 64 percent of the women she interviewed for her book

Women Who Love Sex—another group of easily orgasmic women—
said they had reached orgasm without any kind of touch.

I attended the workshop with an open mind, but no real expec-
tations. I believed spontaneous orgasm could happen, but I didn't really think it would for me.

Surrounded by fifty prone and attentive women, Annie lay on
her back, legs open, her voluminous thin cotton skirt bunched
decorously between bent knees, and demonstrated the fire-breathing
technique. As she sucked in and blew out, imagining her breaths
were arcs of fire coursing through her body in a circle from her
mouth and nose through her genitals, her face contorted and her
body spasmed. She had an orgasm. Or was she faking?

After she caught her breath, Annie led the rest of us in the exercise, borrowed from an American Indian tribe. The woman clos-
est to me started moaning on the first breath. Her significant other is
probably gratified by her instant passion, but I found it intrusive.
Soon the room was filled with the sounds of panting, moaning, and
groaning. It was my first experience with group sex and I hadn't removed my panty hose. Three women said they had orgasms. Had
they only been hyperventilating? Several others reported they came
close to orgasm. How close? I hadn't even achieved an elevated pulse
rate. Was I inept?

Following a break, Annie led us in the exercise again. It produced similar results for me: nothing. I got the names and phone
numbers of the women who claimed success and asked for help.

The first thing they told me to do was think like a man.

We know that men are primarily erotic visualists, aroused by
what they see, while women are supposed to be more aroused by
words and touch. Women who can reach spontaneous orgasm are
capable of vivid visualization. They indulge in torrid, graphic fantasies featuring juicy genital and oral sex and sometimes wild sex
practices such as anal sex, group sex, bondage, or S&M scenarios—
not the kind of misty romantic courtship stories that fade before the
man can take off his pants.

Christine, for instance, lies naked on her bed and imagines her boyfriend making love to her "until I can feel him on my skin and finally inside my body." She does not consciously control or monitor her breathing but begins by taking deep, yoga-style breaths. Well into her fantasies, she may become aware that she's panting, and then the panting "feeds" her arousal.

Lisa credits her ability to reach spontaneous orgasm to a sexually repressed childhood. Fearful of touching herself yet beset by tremendous erotic longings, she fantasized to orgasm. She combines fantasy with breath control. Like Annie Sprinkle, she imagines she is breathing from her genitals and flexes her pubococcygeal, or PC, muscles—the muscles that control the flow of urine—in time with her breathing. Her fantasies include copious amounts of oral sex, both giving and receiving, with men who have beautifully sculptured bodies, in exotic tropical locales. Though she has never made love to a man of a different race, she frequently fantasizes doing so when she's having a no-touch orgasm. "The taboo factor," she says, "excites me so that I don't need touch."

Other women concentrate more on using their PC muscles than breathing. Once Cassie is highly aroused by focusing on mental images of her own body—breasts, vulva, clitoris, thighs—she flexes her muscles in a fast pattern of tense, hold, release, until she brings herself to orgasm. She considers the spontaneous orgasm an ultimate self-loving experience because "you really have to go deep inside yourself to have one."

I quickly saw the pattern of behavior in no-hands women (see page 16) and I challenged myself to use it successfully. By following the directions given me by the orgasmically proficient, I have experienced extended orgasms, multiple orgasms, and extragenital orgasms—from touch to parts of the body other than the genitals, such as breasts, inner thighs, ears, neck. Any woman who is orgasmic can learn to be more so if she is told what to do. Why couldn't this set of instructions work for me, too?

Angie, another workshop participant who hadn't been able to reach orgasm during the class, also believed she could learn the technique.

"As a teenager, I got more out of petting than my partners did: I always came during the full-body clinch that accompanied the good-night kiss at the door," she said. "I have occasional orgasms in my sleep. A former lover told me he thought I could come driving over railroad tracks."

If we can't have a spontaneous orgasm, then who can? we asked each other.

To put myself in the mood, I unplugged the phone, lit gardenia-scented candles, poured a glass of champagne, and filled the tub with bubbles. For half an hour, I sipped and soaked, and allowed my mind to roam freely over my lover's body, first admiring, then desiring him. As I soaped my body in lingering caresses and afterward rubbed my skin with cream, I wondered if I was cheating by granting myself prespontaneous stroking.

Lying naked and anointed on my bed, hands chastely at my sides, I concentrated on breathing deeply, in and out, inhaling through the nose, exhaling through the mouth—like blowing out birthday candles. I imagined having sex with my lover and lost track of my breathing. I started rocking my pelvis back and forth. How I wanted to touch him, no, how I wanted to touch me, because he wasn't there.

I imagined taking him in my mouth. And I felt his mouth surround my clitoris. I flexed my PC muscles tightly and quickly. I wanted that orgasm so badly, I reached for it—with my hand—and began to come seconds after I touched myself. The sensations seemed to last a long time and felt stronger than they would have from masturbation alone.

I never met an orgasm I didn't like and I certainly liked this one. But it wasn't a no-touch orgasm. I called Angie for her progress report. She, too, had "cheated" by using her hands.

"How do you manage not to touch yourself when you're on the verge of orgasm?" I asked the experts, the women who have these spontaneous orgasms.

They weren't, most said, even tempted to touch themselves. As they told me to try harder, *focus* harder, I felt like I was being exhorted to a higher standard of behavior. They reminded me of new mothers who had refused painkillers during delivery, continued breast-feeding through chapped nipples, and prepared their own strained carrots—from organically grown carrots, of course—while I was the equivalent of the woman who'd begged for drugs, substituted bottle for breast, and begun clipping the baby food coupons in the ninth month of pregnancy. They were the Martha Stewarts of orgasm. I was a slacker.

"Pretend you'll burn your fingers if you touch yourself," Lisa said.

Each time I tried to have a spontaneous orgasm, I could not resist touching myself when the desire for orgasm became overwhelming. Then I discovered that I could have a no-hands orgasm shortly after I'd already masturbated to a first orgasm. At that point, when my body is in a state of elevated arousal conducive to multiple orgasms, I, too, can have a no-touch orgasm by flexing my PC muscles and fantasizing my lover's mouth on me. At that point, however, I have also experienced orgasm from arching my back and squeezing my thighs together. Again, I checked with Angie. She'd managed to have a second orgasm without touch, simply by squeezing the thighs as she flexed her PCs and fantasized.

Is it worth the bother?

Orgasm is *never* a bother. Any quest for sexual fulfillment that involves no risk of rejection, no exposure to sexually transmitted diseases, and no morning-after regrets can't be a bad thing. I don't think I will spend much time trying to have a no-touch orgasm in the future, but I will employ the breathing techniques and allow myself more active fantasy time before I begin to masturbate or even sometimes before I make love. By fantasizing more, employing a new breathing technique, flexing my PC muscles like mad, and delaying touch, I had stronger orgasms than I typically experience during masturbation or intercourse alone—even if I didn't achieve the goal.

"It was worth it for me, too," Angie agreed. "I see that my PCs need strengthening, for one thing. Also, I think using the breathing and flexing techniques during intercourse makes my orgasm better."

Can you have a spontaneous orgasm?

It isn't as easy as the word *spontaneous* implies, but it is possible, provided you already indulge in X-rated fantasies.

"Hot fantasies are the key element," said one woman who has successfully mastered the technique. "If you can't make them really hot, you can't do it."

And why shouldn't you try? Whether you have an orgasm without touch or find you can arouse yourself to a fever pitch through fantasy alone, you will learn something about your body and its responses, information you can use in masturbation or in lovemaking. You may also discover that locked inside your brain is the ability to fantasize wild and wonderful sexual scenarios you'd never dream of acting out.

Why not have fun while building the long desire?

How to Have a No-Touch Orgasm, Hers

- Establish an erotic mood, as you would for masturbation or lovemaking. Use music, candles, a bubble bath, wine, sexy clothing—whatever it takes to make you feel sexy. Turn yourself on.

- Create lush, passionate fantasies. If you don't typically fantasize graphic sexual scenarios, read erotica to establish the mood.

- Practice breath control lying on your back, knees bent, feet spaced well apart. Start with *deep breaths*. Pull your breath into your body so deeply you feel your diaphragm expanding and can imagine air going all the way down to your genitals. When you breathe out, pull that air all the way out, again imagining you are drawing it up through your genitals into your body. After a dozen or so deep breaths, *pant*. Breathe rapidly from your belly with your mouth open. Now use the *fire-breathing* technique. Begin with relaxing shallow breaths. Then breathe deeply. Inhale through the nose, exhale through the mouth. Make the breathing continuous or circular. Imagine a circle of fire beginning first as a small circle, nose through mouth, then expanding to include chest, belly, and finally genitals. Feel the erotic heat moving in a circle throughout your body as you breathe.

• Flex the PC muscles either alone or in combination with the breathing. The PC muscles also control the flow of urine. You can locate them and practice flexing—tense, hold, release—while urinating. Coordinate your flexing with deep breathing. Switch to panting, then to deep breathing, finally to fire-breathing while flexing, if you can manage this. (It may take practice to fire-breathe and flex all at once.)

Success depends heavily on the strength of your PC muscles. In fact, you will find this to be true of many techniques in this book. To strengthen those muscles, and your orgasms, practice kegels, a set of simple exercises. (For directions, see page 109.)

*T*HE ULTIMATE SEXUAL HEAD TRIP FOR MEN ONLY: THE E TECHNIQUE

Men can think themselves to orgasm, too, according to Graham Masterton, the noted English sexologist who has written two of the all-time best-selling sex books, *How to Drive Your Woman Wild in Bed* and *How to Drive Your Man Wild in Bed,* and was also reputedly "M," the mysterious author of *The Sensuous Man,* the 1971 follow-up to the hugely successful *The Sensuous Woman* by "J."

"Why would a man want to do that?" I asked him. "Wouldn't that be like thinking yourself to premature ejaculation?"

On a typically gloomy London afternoon, we were having tea in a little shop not far from Kensington Palace, where Princess Diana resides. I was, I confess, biased in favor of the female spontaneous experience. Anything that helps a woman get aroused faster is good. But why would we want to encourage men to hurry themselves along? I asked the inventor of the E technique. Shouldn't they clench their buttocks, think of England, and hold on as long as possible?

"Trying to reach a climax without physical stimulus teaches a man to fine-tune his mental control over his penis," Masterton said patiently. "Rather than encouraging him to ejaculate quickly as masturbation does, the E technique—for ejaculation—teaches him to take his time along the arousal path."

If you can literally think your way to a climax, then you can think your way into not ejaculating, too. But is that possible? Doesn't male physiology require direct penile stimulation?

"Well," he conceded, "you hold it in your hand, but absolutely no stroking."

None?

"Some of the men I've taught this method report they've had to trigger ejaculation by tugging down on the penis or inserting a finger in the anus or even using two or three masturbatory hand strokes. That's not cheating. A few strokes won't affect the psychosexual training."

Back home in the States, I gave Masterton's written directions to several male friends. Three out of seven were able to ejaculate ten to fifteen minutes into the E technique with minimal touching after seven or eight tries, a number of tries which Masterton says is "typical of the learning process." They reported intense, highly satisfying orgasms. The other four got bored or frustrated and gave up after two or three tries.

One slacker said, "I may have learned something about my penis, but I'm not sure."

Later, he called me back and added: "I think I may have been uncomfortable with the process. Women are encouraged to create sensuous environments for themselves. Men aren't. I felt a little like a sissyboy lighting my candle and putting my music on, not for a woman, but only for me."

Another man, who is forty and recently divorced, said, "I gained some control over the ejaculatory process, which is a more important goal for me than learning to think myself to orgasm. I don't have the time for that!"

Two men who weren't able to make the technique work for them asked me to relay specific advice from those who had more success.

Ryan suggested: "I tried the E technique while lying flat on my back the first six times. I finally got it to work by lying on my side. The pressure of my thighs against my genitals helped. The climax definitely felt great."

And Bill said, "Perfecting this technique did give me better mental control over the arousal process. And it forced me to get those PC muscles in shape, something I always thought was for women only. That helped a lot and made my orgasms in general a lot stronger. The intensity of that E technique orgasm, however, really knocked me out. The head of my cock felt like it was exploding. I was seeing stars.

"I'll bet most guys who failed didn't do their kegels. You know how men are: We think we don't need to read the directions all the way through."

Yes, the two men who'd wanted advice said that Bill was right. They hadn't done their kegels. ("I really thought kegels were for women," one said. "Then I tried them. Real macho stuff.")

The good news, according to Masterton, is that even a small degree of success with the E technique will turn a man into a more skillful lover.

"You will find that you can delay your climax or speed it up simply by selecting the right fantasy, the right degree of concentration, and by complementing that mental concentration with a high degree of awareness of what is happening inside your own genitals."

How to have an almost no-touch orgasm, his

- Relax. Take a shower, have a glass of wine, put on some music. Lie naked on your bed. "Think of the women to whom you'd like to make love," Masterton said. "Think of the women to whom you have made love—but only the wonderful ones."

- Hold your penis lightly in one hand, with your finger and thumb around the head. You may press the frenum, or the ridge surrounding the head, lightly with the tip of your index fingers. That extra contact might help you feel the changes in hardness taking place as your fantasies wax and wane.

- Fantasize the most wildly erotic scenarios you can imagine. Don't censor yourself. "Have no inhibitions in your fantasies and you will be able to quickly arouse yourself to full erection," he says. "If your mind wanders, you will lose your erection, so the fantasies must be extraordinary."

- Keep the hand holding your penis still. No rubbing, stroking, or squeezing.

- As your arousal grows, squeeze your PC muscles. Try combinations of long and short squeezes to see what works best for you. (See directions for kegels, exercises for men to strengthen the PC muscles, page 109.) Keep flexing them as you imagine yourself building up to a tremendous climax.

- Focus your mental energy on the head of your penis. See it and feel it ejaculating in your mind's eye. (You may need to take a few gentle squeezes to ejaculate, but the less you can touch your penis, the better.)

Chapter Two

SAY IT LIKE YOU WANT IT

*K*aren and her husband have demanding jobs as regional sales directors for different companies. She travels three weeks a month, he two or three weeks a month. They have, she told me, perfected the art of phone sex, an erotic skill they developed after she read the novel about phone sex, *Vox,* by Nicholson Baker.

"'What are you wearing?' he always asks first," she said. "I tell him I'm wearing something good, like a big black silk shirt and nothing else, even if I'm wrapped in the terry-cloth robe supplied by the hotel."

Very clever of Karen. Men need to see the erotic in a clear way. To prepare him for phone sex, Karen even packs lingerie she won't wear so he can visualize her in the wispy pieces of silk and lace he's watched her tuck into her carry-on bag. Before she figured this out, Karen once told him over the phone that she was wearing a sweater and tights.

"He couldn't get aroused," she said. "He told me, 'No, that doesn't do it for me. Take off the tights.' I told him I had though I hadn't."

After he has a good visual image of Karen in her erotic finery, he will ask, "What are you doing?"

"I'll say something like 'I'm holding the phone with my left hand. My right hand is resting between my legs on top of my mons. One finger is poised, ready to slip inside if I so much as wiggle my hips.'

"'Are you wet?' he'll ask.

"'Yes, I am wet,' I'll tell him. 'When I part my lips, I will be sitting in a pool of moisture, aching for you.'

"Then he'll say something like 'I love your wetness. I want to touch you, put my face into you, feel your liquid running down my chin. . . .'

"Then I am wet. It's easy to go on from there."

Karen's husband says things to her over the phone when they are a great distance apart that he doesn't say when they are entwined in each other's arms. Perhaps distance takes away the last trace of his inhibition about speaking of his feelings. Or perhaps he subconsciously uses language more effectively when he cannot use his other attributes to give her pleasure.

"It isn't only the words," she said. "His voice changes, deepens and cascades over my body. Prolonged silences are heavy with desire communicated through breathing. A clearing of his throat or a sigh can sometimes catch in my groin and make my clitoris begin to vibrate like a tuning fork at low pitch."

Words and the sounds and silences accompanying them can be a form of sexplay. Through your verbal skills, you can bring a partner, and yourself, to a higher state of arousal whether you're together in the same bed or thousands of miles apart. Sexually explicit language—one form of erotic noise—can electrify a sexual encounter, taking it out of the ordinary and into the extraordinary.

Many men love "dirty talk." They want their partners to beg, "Lick my pussy" and "Let me suck your big hard cock." Some women wrinkle their noses in distaste at the thought of uttering, "Rub the head of your cock across my clit." Others use graphic sex talk to excite their partners and themselves—and find the experience thrilling, even liberating. How important is aural sex?

Bob Berkowitz, the popular host of CNBC's highly rated talk show *Real Personal,* says, "Based on mail and calls to the show, I would say that the desire to hear a woman talk 'dirty' is almost as high up on the male wish list as oral sex."

How to Talk Like a Bad Girl

- Don't feel guilty about dirty talk. A Manhattan trophy wife, whose name regularly appears in the gossip columns as hostess of one or another gala function, told me she got her husband away from his first wife by "talking dirty and swallowing." You may disdain this trophy wife—or any woman who gets what she wants through the dispensing of sexual favors—but on some level, in some way, each of us makes accommodations in a relationship in order to get the other person to meet our needs. You want great sex—and you know that great sex happens when two people do what excites and pleasures the other. You can use your voice to arouse him just as you use your mouth, lips, tongue, hands, and body.

- Learn the words. Erotic novels are filled with euphemisms for genitals and their interactions. For example: *He plunged into her, his cock slipping neatly into the soft, thick wetness of her aching cunt.* Say the words out loud. But if you can't say the graphic words, use words more comfortable for you, such as *penis* rather than *cock.* Which words turn you on? Which make you feel like a bad girl—a good feeling? Read them to your partner. Work the exciting ones into sentences.

- Rent movies you consider erotic—and *listen* to them. Wear a blindfold if you must to keep from watching. Make note of the dialogue in both mainstream R-rated films and X-rated videos that arouse you. Borrow that dialogue. Pretend you are an actor and use the words with your lover.

Once you are comfortable saying the words as a scriptwriter wrote them, you can personalize them to make it sound more like you speaking.

• Call a phone sex service, even if you're a heterosexual woman and the operators are all women. The charge will be between twenty and fifty dollars for their hottest scenarios. Ask, "What do you say to turn a man on?" or "What scene do men most often ask you to play out?"

• Read erotica out loud. If you are uncomfortable reading out loud to your partner, practice alone. Hearing the language of arousal and lovemaking in your own voice will increase your comfort level. You might discover that hearing erotic passages spoken in your own voice makes them more exciting.

A CONVERSATION AT FOUR DOLLARS A MINUTE

Call her Mandy. Her specialty is whatever you want, hot sex, any way you like. Her real name is Michelle, her family calls her Mikey, but she tells the callers, "Call me Mandy—and do keep calling."

"I don't make money if I'm not talking," she said. "I can talk sexy in a sweatsuit, with cotton balls between my toes while the polish is drying."

The male callers don't see the cotton balls, of course, not even in their fantasies. They picture Mandy with long blond hair, big blue eyes, long, long legs ending in feet with scarlet-painted toes, and size 38C breasts. She is really a petite woman with short brown hair who wears little makeup and "doesn't need to wear" a bra, but she has a sultry voice that says, *blond, legs, boobs.*

"The callers always ask, 'What do you look like?' and 'What are you wearing?'" she said, "because men are visual. They get the mental picture of me before they begin doing things to me in their heads."

If more women talked dirty, Mandy believes, she would make less money.

"Men love the idea of a woman saying those words only for them. Their wives and girlfriends won't say those things. I tell them I am young and blond and busty, because that's what they want. Young, for not too experienced. Blond, for angelic. It would be no thrill to hear those words from the lips of a street hooker. Busty, well, you know for what."

What are the favorite scenarios?

"Oral and anal. They want me to suck them off or they want to fuck my ass. In real life, my boyfriend wants anal sex at least once a week, whereas my limit is once a month. Sometimes I will talk him through the anal fantasy while we're having intercourse. That really works for him. Other women could make it work for their men, too."

Mandy learned her trade by first listening to other phone sex operators, then practicing on the phone with her boyfriend.

"If you aren't comfortable with dirty talk, start on the phone," she advised. "Just leave a hot message on his voice mail, like 'Baby, I'm thinking about you right now. I want to put my lips around your hard cock. I want to run my tongue along the ridge at the base of the head.'

"Make it specific. Men want to hear the details. That's why it's easier to start with a phone message. A lot of women are too shy to say more than a few lines. Then, when you feel good with that, you call him some night and tell him you want to talk about sexual fantasies. Make up something that you know will turn him on, and again, make it hot and specific. And they want to hear big talk, like 'I feel your cock inside me. You're so big. You fill me up like I've never been filled before.'

"And they want to hear you beg to be fucked. Say, 'I want you so bad. I want you to fuck me so hard, please fuck me hard.'

"Play to their hidden fantasies. Men want to ejaculate on a woman's body, or they think they do, but they wouldn't ask their woman to let them do that. They want to see themselves come and they want to feel totally accepted by their women.

"Say, 'I want you to come all over my breasts. I want to rub your hot creamy cum into my tits.'

"And swallowing. That's a big desire for men. Say, 'I want you to come in my mouth. I want to taste and feel you shooting down my throat. I want to swallow you, baby.'

"Pretend you're masturbating for him. Say, 'I'm touching myself now. My fingers are playing with my lips. I'm stroking my clit. Ooh, oh, that feels so good'—Don't forget to pant and gasp!—'Now I have one finger up my pussy and the other one on my clit. I'm rubbing it.'

"If he's ever admitted to fantasies or desires you don't want to bring to reality in your bed, use them in hot fantasy talk. Like having sex with two women. Say, 'Oh, baby, she's licking my cunt. I have her tit in my hand. She's rubbing against me, baby. Can you see us together? Does it make you hot?'

"Or call him and pretend you're the woman in the next apartment building and you have your drapes open and you're undressing and he should undress, too.

"If you have trouble thinking what to say, buy some dirty books or magazines and read the juicy parts. That works when you're with him, too. The sex magazines print letters about anal sex. Memorize one so you can talk that scene while he's making love to you. Or pretend someone is watching you have sex. You describe the other person and how he or she is acting while your man is making love to you. If it's a man watching, he's getting hard, and if it's a woman, she's masturbating.

"I promise you'll have a really hot time."

Remember *Arabian Nights,* the story of Scheherazade and the 1,001 nights? The captive Scheherazade kept herself alive by telling the king a different erotic story each night. She wove fact and fantasy together to keep him spellbound until at last he was her emotional captive and she his bride. Mandy made me think of Scheherazade.

$\mathcal{T}$HE EROTIC READING CIRCLE:
ELEVEN WOMEN AND A DIRTY BOOK

If your tastes run to more literate erotica, consider forming a reading circle.

Some book discussion groups don't exchange opinions on the meaning of a novel by Anthony Trollope or John Updike. A group of heterosexual women in San Francisco have been meeting once a month for the past two years to read aloud from erotic books or sometimes from poetry and graphic magazine pieces. According to the "facilitator," Darla, a petite blond executive in her mid-thirties, the size of the group varies from five or six to more than twenty, ranging in age from the early twenties to early fifties.

Darla and two other women, who have since relocated to other cities, formed the reading group as an "antidote to the new prissiness sweeping the San Francisco area and the nation.

"We walked into a women's bookstore together one evening after having dinner together downtown. We saw a small circle surrounding an author reading from her work so we moved to the edge of the circle. It was lesbian erotica. We aren't titillated by lesbian erotica, so we moved away.

"Later, Jane said, 'You would never see a reading of heterosexual erotica in this or any bookstore—unless it was Anne Rice, because she's big enough to get away with anything. There's little support for heterosexual erotica in the women's movement.'

"I said, 'Why don't we start our own reading group for heterosexual women who want to read erotica?'

"We laughed and shrugged it off. But the next time we had dinner, Jane said, 'Why not?' and so we did.

"Authors range from John Keats and Percy Shelley to Anne Rice and some romance novelists and those little paperback books you find in the smut section of your local bookstore," she explained to me over the phone. Lowering her voice dramatically, she added, "We even read *porn*."

Why do they get together to read aloud? Under the guise of "expanding our knowledge of erotic literature"—in Darla's words—they turn each other, and themselves, on. Do they go home in a state of arousal to waiting partners? If not, do they find release at their own fingertips? Yes and yes.

At the meeting I attended, eleven attractive well-dressed women from twenty-one through forty-seven sat in the living room of a spacious apartment decorated down to the cacti in Southwest style. Each held a copy of the trade paperback edition of *The New Olympia Reader,* edited by Maurice Girodias. Originally published in 1970, *The Reader* is a collection of erotic writings from the 1960s with contributions by Diane di Prima, Jack Kerouac's lover, and William Burroughs, among others. The cover, a waist-down shot of a woman clad in lacy bloomers and thigh-high fishnet stockings, is demure yet provocative, making it an apt choice for these women wearing business suits with short skirts and high heels.

"'Our tongues were jousting now in a fine fencing match of pleasure, touching and tilting as we moved slightly from side to side in our attempts to bring our flesh into more and more total contact,'" Darla began reading with an excerpt from di Prima's "Memoirs of a Beatnik." "'I slid a knee up under his balls and rotated it gently, while examining his entire palate with the tip of my tongue. In reply, he pressed one thigh awkwardly against my crotch, just touching my clitoris . . .'"

Apparently Darla wasn't the only one who liked erotica, which reads like a jazzed-up sex instruction manual. I saw nipples become erect under silk blouses. Here and there a flush spread across a pale cheek. Two women uncrossed their legs, squirmed a bit in their chairs, and recrossed them.

"'My tongue briefly played with his hard slight nipples . . .'" Darla continued.

In my mind's eye, I saw my lover, whose little nipples like smooth pebbles are exquisitely sensitive. I watched his body jerk in a spasm of pleasure as I rolled one nipple between my tongue and teeth. And I understood why these women gathered together to read out loud from dirty books. As one after another read favored passages, I experienced their words and the inflections they chose to convey their meaning as ocean breezes floating my fantasy sailboat on a sexual sea. When they spoke of muscles rippling in a man's back, of masculine hands caressing female flesh, I saw the flesh I knew or coveted and was transported. They put a fresh soundtrack to my favorite old fantasies—and gave me some new ones. I was, in fact, more easily able to put myself into spoken erotica than into, for example, an X-rated video, which might arouse me, but not in this personal way.

During a break in the reading, I asked the women sitting next to me if they had also put themselves into the story as it was being read. They had.

"Listening to someone else read is like being taken on an erotic cruise," said a flamboyant auburn-haired public-relations consultant in her late thirties. "You visit these exotic mental ports of call you wouldn't imagine on your own."

And Christie, an attorney who has belonged to the group from the start, said, "I get ideas from the readings sometimes. Like that nipple thing. I was listening and wondering if the new man in my life has sensitive nipples and how he would respond if I played with them. Other times the readings are about things which excite me that I'd never do, like S&M. It's thrilling to listen to. Watching videos of S&M is too heavy. I can't handle that."

The reading continued with "The Ordeal of the Rod," another selection from *The New Olympia Reader,* which led to a spirited and intelligent discussion of the appeal of dominance and submission themes. The consensus was that such stories give a variety of voices to the rape fantasy, a universal fantasy among men as well as women. The rape fantasy indicates a desire to have sex without guilt, not a desire to be raped. The one woman who found the material offensive said she feared she did so because of "unacknowledged and repressed feelings in that area."

"After we read that chapter from *The Story of O,* I had such hot sex with Ken I was too embarrassed to tell him what we'd been reading," said Kelly, a slender brunette karate instructor in her late twenties. "I didn't want him to think I was really into sadomasochism."

"What did you tell him we'd been reading?" asked Darla, a chocolate truffle ready to pop into her mouth.

"The letters from *Penthouse Forum*," Kelly said. "What he wants to hear."

The women exploded in barking laughter as the tray of chocolates was passed around. The refreshments at each meeting have to be chocolate and "sexy," with the favorites being chocolate truffles, cream-filled eclairs, and—I'm stumped by this one, not that they aren't delicious—Entenmann's low-fat chocolate-covered doughnuts. The chocolate is washed down by flavored coffees, champagne, and sherry.

"There's nothing like an evening of chocolate, champagne, and dirty books to improve your sex life," joked a married woman in her thirties. "My husband thinks this group is the best thing that's ever happened to me."

All eleven women declared the group a positive influence on their sex lives. Many gave the obvious reason: They went home in a state of arousal to an eagerly waiting partner. Almost as often, they said they were more comfortable about their fantasies now that they knew other "normal" women shared them.

"This is the only place I go where it is okay to be openly sexual," said Christie. "Women are so judgmental of one another everywhere else. And public discourse about sex is all negative. Sexual harassment, sex abuse, sexual exploitation of women, and so forth. This group revs my engines. I feel good about being a sexual woman when I leave here. In today's world, I need that reinforcement."

Why don't they read at home alone or to their men? Some of them do. And they say it is a different experience from the one they have at group. Others, like Kelly, who claimed never to "indulge" outside the circle, seem to need permission from the group to indulge in erotica.

Why would reading with a lover be a "different experience"?

Maybe for the same reason an orgasm achieved through masturbation can feel more intense than one reached during lovemaking. In the reading group, women aren't distracted by thoughts of their partners. They aren't monitoring his responses or consciously trying to arouse him more by the tone of their voices or the passages they choose. And they don't have to feel self-conscious about their own responses.

"When I read with my lover," one woman said, "I use the material as an erotic aide. The point is to get us excited, to make the sex better. When I read alone or in the safety of this group, the point is not to have a point. I can see what I like without feeling pressure to like what he likes or what I think he thinks I should like."

"It's politically incorrect to like this stuff," Darla said. "Who tells you hot sex is good these days? Sex is taboo again. That excites me. I don't know about everyone else. But I go home feeling like a wanton woman, something I don't have the courage to be in real life."

Hot sex is *not* PC. Though "political correctness" may be finished as a popular construct, the concept still maintains a hold on minds in San Francisco, where PC was born. And the new prissiness does seem to have settled like a stagnant weather front over the nation.

Ah, the sweet frisson of excitement generated by the breaking of taboos.

The Group's Top Ten

Nonfiction: *Sex: An Oral History,* by Harry Maurer; *The Best Sex I Ever Had: Real People Recall Their Most Erotic Experiences,* by Steve and Iris Finz; *The Erotic Impulse: Honoring the Sensual Self,* edited by David Steinberg; *Sex Lives,* by Mark Baker.

Collection: *Yellow Silk: Erotic Arts and Letters,* edited by Lily Pond and Richard Russo.

Fiction: *Vox,* by Nicholson Baker; *Fear of Flying,* by Erica Jong; *The Lover,* by Marguerite Duras; *9 1/2 Weeks,* by Elizabeth McNeill; *The Autobiography of My Body,* by David Guy.

How to Form an Erotic Reading Circle

• Limit the reading material to erotica. After the group is established, you may want to include a mainstream novel that has one or two great bedroom scenes. In the beginning, keep your focus.

• Limit the membership to women who want to read erotica and expand their erotic libraries. ("These women may not be your best friends," Darla says. "Put an ad in a city paper or magazine to get women on the same wavelength.") Make it clear to prospective members that anti-porn activism won't be tolerated.

• Let one person be the facilitator for a period of six months to a year. ("At first, we tried to be too casual, with no one in charge," Darla says. "That didn't work, because someone has to be responsible for getting the meeting information out to people who missed the last meeting or it doesn't get done.") The facilitator can also assign duties, such as buying the doughnuts.

• At each meeting, ask for suggested books for the next meeting. Anyone who proposes a book must have buying information—and copies of reviews if there are any. The members vote on the suggested selections.

• Set aside time for socializing before and after the reading.

EROTIC NOISES

The category is not limited to the kind of "uhms" that punctuate a Donna Summers song or the sounds Meg Ryan made during the world's most famous faked orgasm, in *When Harry Met Sally.* In a wooded retreat high in the northern California mountains, I met with Rahula Surkang, who teaches "The Ecstatic Sounds of Sex," a workshop in erotic noises.

The sense of hearing is important both to the sex act and to the act of seduction—and perhaps more important in these regards to women than men. What woman has not been seduced by the right words spoken in a rich male voice? Instinctively we know that men are primarily seduced by visuals and women by words. We each respond in our own way to the combination of tone, pitch, and rhythm in other voices, but women respond more strongly than men do to the beloved's voice, which is why phone sex must be filled with visual cues for him.

And the physical sounds of lovemaking are an essential part of the act for most people. Have you ever been with someone who didn't make much noise? A character in D. H. Lawrence's classic novel *Lady Chatterley's Lover* found such silence "fathomless" and begged her partner to reassure her of his love. He was "so much more peaceful in love than she" that she needed to be told repeatedly "I love you."

The connection between sex and music is as old as mankind. The erotic power of the voice accompanied by music has been celebrated throughout history from the myth of the Sirens who lured sailors to their death to the modern celebrity status of rock singers. Music can be profoundly erotic, whether that music is created with instruments or by birds. Yes, birds.

"Do you mean some people need a class in moaning and sighing?" a friend asked when I told her about the erotic noises workshop. "Are they going to teach you how to sing? I don't think we can all learn how to sing."

No, not moaning and sighing, which comes naturally, and not singing, which doesn't—*erotic noises,* a varied soundtrack to accompany, enhance, even intensify sex. Based on ancient sex traditions, the aural techniques and their appeal to some people are difficult to describe. The workshop participants are not those couples in which one or the other complains of a silent partner. The people who pay five hundred to one thousand dollars—depending on whether they opt for the bed and the all-natural foods and no-caffeine breakfast or merely the training sessions—want their lovemaking to sound like a flock of birds on hormones is roosting in their rafters. Are birdsongs really such a strange accompaniment to lovemaking?

"The voice of man has power, but so do the voices of birds," Rahula believes.

Perhaps birdsongs evoke memories of lovemaking in open fields, memories buried like a microchip in our subconscious minds.

"In *The Tibetan Treatise on Passion*," Rahula explained, "we are taught that there are eight sounds of passion. Each sound is based on the voice of a different bird."

He handed me the book written by the late Gedun Chopel, the former monk whom many consider to be Tibet's foremost intellect of the twentieth century. In the early part of this century, Chopel traveled to India and learned Sanskrit to study the *Kama Sutra,* which he adapted in the *Treatise.* His twin goals were increasing female sexual pleasure and enhancing male and female spirituality by elevating sexual pleasure to the level of ecstasy. And ecstasy is not a quiet state.

At first glance, the description of the sounds looked suspiciously like a soundtrack for rough sex.

For example, number one reads: "He beats her rear with the pangs of passion. She embraces him and puts her mouth to his; from inside the throat she emits the sound 'noo.' This sound is called the voice of the pigeon."

"What are we talking about here?" I asked Rahula. "Erotic spanking?"

He frowned gently, pursed his lips, and said, "Noo." Making the sounds, he explained, frees something inside us. "It loosens the grip of tension on the erotic sensibility. Hearing the sounds stirs our passions. They call to us in a secret language we didn't know we understood until we heard it spoken."

In other words, you can't take the descriptions too literally. The eight sounds are:

The "noo."

The voice of the kokila, the "hoo" sound, elicited when the man touches the tip of his "jewel" to the tip of her womb.

The voice of the peacock. Crying and shouting noises, like a cat falling down a ravine, induced by strong pangs of unbearable passion.

The pleasant tone of a bee's sucking honey. A hissed "sa si" of unspeakable bliss. (Chopel neglected to say how one induces it, a curious omission.)

The voice of a goose, the low sound of a bell, when "timidity is pierced through by passion," or the point where shyness gives way to desire and one begs to be touched, stroked, loved.

The voice of a quail, the cry made when the penis enters the vagina.

The voice of a black goose, the ravenous gasps of furious intercourse.

The voice of the dove, the post-orgasmic coo.

After demonstrating the sounds for me and refreshing us both with herbal tea, Rahula invited me to hear a session in which four couples were perfecting their penetration sounds. He directed me to sit behind a paneled wood screen painted with birds so that I would not violate their privacy or be distracted by "visual aides," such as appearance or animation of gestures.

"I want you to focus only on the sounds," he said. "Then tell me if you can envision the acts that would accompany the sounds. Tell me if you can feel these acts of love taking place on your body as you listen."

Behind the screen, I sat in a straight-backed chair with no arms, closed my eyes, and listened. A cacophony of bird noises assaulted my ears. I couldn't distinguish one clearly from another and none made me picture a man penetrating a woman in the act of love. Was I hearing "coo" or "hoo" or "noo"? Was that the sound of the quail or the black goose or that other goose, presumably white? I felt as if I were trapped in a duck blind with an avid hunter waiting for the birds to stop mating and fly away so that he could fairly shoot them.

I wanted to take his gun away and shoot them myself—and I've never shot at anything but a target or skeet.

"Were you overwhelmed by the sounds?" Rahula asked me afterward.

"Yes," I could honestly reply. "I was."

He gave me a cassette, a recording of the full panoply of sounds, to take home. I didn't get around to playing it for days, and when I did, I was stunned at the beauty, the erotic quality of the "noises." Obviously these makers of erotic noise had been properly trained in the voices of birds. Soothing at first, the sounds grew in intensity, gripping me with their sexual urgency. I played the tape while masturbating, then while making love. Later, my lover and I tried to make our own bird sounds and produced nothing erotic.

I called Rahula and asked, "What did we do wrong?"

"Some people," he said, "will be very aroused by making the sounds themselves. To someone listening as you were listening behind the screen, the sounds may not be arousing. Other people will be aroused by hearing the sounds perfectly made—like a symphony played by fine musicians—as you and your partner were aroused. They won't need or want to make the sounds themselves.

"It is not important that you can make bird sounds. It is more important that you can open yourself up to the erotic quality of sounds, and the tape helped you do that." After a slight pause, he added, "It was also good for you to find amusement in what the couples were doing while you were sitting behind the screen. I encourage people to find amusement in sex. If we cannot laugh and have fun, we cannot have real passion, either."

A few days later, a couple who had participated in the workshop called, at Rahula's request, to describe their experience for me.

"Making those sounds freed something inside me," the man said. "I have been too closed to erotic possibilities. These exercises seem to me like a softer and more erotic version of that scream therapy that was popular years ago, though I am guessing, because I didn't have that therapy."

"We were conventional in our lovemaking," his partner added.

"We aren't so conventional anymore. I can't tell you why this has worked for us, but it has. We found the tapes interesting, but not as exciting as making the sounds ourselves."

You can find the tapes or similar ones in many shops selling New Age items. Try one. If you find it arousing, then expand your tapes of sexual sounds to include ambient music, recordings of the rain or the ocean or desert winds, nature sounds that make you feel like you're making love outdoors.

$\mathcal{T}$HE LIMITS OF TALK

By coincidence—or through karma?—shortly after returning home from Rahula's retreat, I received a call from a friend who had become briefly involved with a man who preferred at that point in his life to have phone sex over the real thing. He did not want to "cheat" on his fiancée, and she, having similar feelings of her own about a new man in her life, was comfortable with that.

Yet he compared phone sex to radio—"a more intimate form of communication than television." Were they being true to their hearts or were they being somehow more intimate with each other than with their beloveds? Or was he a phone sex fetishist? Whatever his motives, she readily agreed to the game because "he has the voice for phone sex—or radio—deep, undeniably masculine, rich with the resonant tones that promise roiling testosterone," she said. "His voice excited me.

"The first call was the best. 'I want you to stroke your breast,' he said minutes into our conversation, 'and imagine that it is my hand.' I put my right hand over my left breast and squeezed, my fingertips creating whorls of pleasurable pressure. 'Stroke,' he said, as if he could see, 'not squeeze.'

"I took the hand away and stroked, with one finger, then two, short, then wide, sweeping motions, down the sides, big circles growing smaller around the nipples.

"'Stroke,' he soothed. 'Tell me how it feels.'

"'Good,'" I said, pitching my voice lower. 'But I want more.'

"'Let your hand move down your body. My hand is moving down my body now. I'm touching my chest. I have a lot of hair on my chest. You have your hands in my chest hair. Your fingernails are grazing my skin. Ooh, that feels good. Lower, baby, lower.'

"'I want your tongue,' I told him. 'Your tongue to follow your hands down my body. I want your tongue, yes, there, licking the tops of my thighs in the creases where the legs meet the ass. Oh, yes, it's so sensitive there.'

"'Uhm, baby, you taste so good,'" he said. 'Your skin is like silk under my tongue. . . .'

"He took me on an intensely pleasurable journey that day. Great orgasms sucked my fingers, pulling them deeper into the center of one spasm where I would find the beginning of another. There were several more calls, less thrilling than the first.

"After a few weeks, however, I stopped taking his calls altogether," she confessed, "not because I was bored with the game, but because I wanted to feel, or believe I could soon feel, what I had come to know through words alone.

"This wasn't going anywhere. I didn't really want it to go anywhere, but I couldn't get excited about him if it wasn't."

For most of us, the words have to lead to something besides a phone bill.

Chapter Three

THE ART OF THE TEASE

I lived for a while on a very high floor in a Manhattan apartment building. Though it was possible for me to see into apartments across the street, several of the tenants seldom pulled their shades. This is fairly common behavior for urban residents of high-rise buildings, accustomed to being jammed on sidewalks and into subway cars with strangers with whom we do not make eye contact.

"I didn't own shades when I lived on the thirty-seventh floor," a friend said. "Sometimes I masturbated knowing that a man across the way was watching me through binoculars. The act was intimate yet anonymous. His watching emboldened me. In performing for him, I aroused myself to a greater pitch."

Several women who work for a well-known magazine confessed to watching a man who walks around his apartment, visible from their office, in various stages of undress. While he never looks at them, they think he knows they're looking at him and "enjoys" teasing them. I had the same feeling about a couple across the street from my apartment whom I sometimes spied making love.

One night I watched my neighbor seduce her lover. He was obviously lying on the bed, out of my view. She stood in the doorway clad in black bra and tap pants. Even from a distance, her gaze smoldered. Slowly she unhooked the front clasp of her bra and held the parts tantalizingly together with her hands before letting them fall, freeing the pale bouncy breasts, which she deliberately swung by leaning slightly forward, taunting him. She slid the straps off her shoulders and let the bra fall to the floor. With legs apart and eyes on him, she massaged her nipples with the flats of her hands.

She opened her lips and moistened them with her tongue. Then she took one hand away from her breast, licked her fingertips, and let the hand drift at a titillating pace down into her tap pants. Throwing back her head, she masturbated for a few minutes until she walked toward the bed, her breasts bobbing sweetly, enticingly up and down.

I don't have any idea what she did for a living, but she could have made a lot of money in tips if she'd been an exotic dancer.

That woman knew how to tease—something people in relationships have often stopped doing so long ago they can't remember when. Some people believe that sex within the committed relationship should be a straightforward experience, two naked bodies coming together in a state of intimacy so pristine they could be posing for a layout in a story on sex in a holistic health magazine. Teasing makes one feel naughty and dangerous and in control.

Maybe I will and maybe I won't, the tease says, *but if I will, I'll do it when I want, when I know you truly yearn for me.* Teasing is an integral part of erotic play, not a technique to be abandoned once an "open and honest relationship" has been established. The sexual tease is a love game for grown-ups, a game that has two components—visual and physical. Each serves to prolong the initial (and sometimes more intense) stages of arousal, thus prolonging the pleasure for both parties.

THE VISUAL TEASE

This bears repeating because it is the one critical fact about men that women often forget or downplay in importance: Men are erotic visualists, primarily aroused by what they see. A man is initially aroused through his eyes.

"Invitational dressing" is Graham Masterton's term for giving a man small but obvious clues about your intentions and desires through your choice of clothing. Lace-topped stockings rather than panty hose on a date. Soft silk blouses with the buttons unfastened to the top of the cleavage. High heels, preferably sling-backs or sandals. Body-caressing knits. Sometimes men misread those clues. And sometimes we practice invitational dressing without meaning to invite or entice. We just like the look. There's nothing wrong with that. Men can handle a little visual stimulation that isn't going to take them anywhere. We don't have to dress like Puritans to keep their minds off sex.

The best visual tease is an invitation, not an aggressive demand.

"Nothing is sexier than a woman in an oversized man's white shirt and nothing else," said my friend Bob.

"I love it when a woman goes braless beneath her clothes," said Ken, "but I don't like anything that shows too clearly she's braless. You should have to look to see her breasts moving under her clothing. Catching a glimpse of a nipple hardening is so much more exciting than having that nipple outlined by a tight sheer fabric. And I hate black bras or no bras under transparent blouses. When a woman dresses like that, she's intimidating."

"The way women dress and walk and move is all part of healthy sexual play," said Keith, a therapist. "Most people know by now that leaning forward when you're speaking to someone can be a form of courtship behavior, as can touching an arm or hand while speaking or tossing back the hair or flicking off the piece of imaginary lint from the other person's shoulder."

These forms of light teasing all but disappear after the consummation. Often women also stop dressing provocatively for their men, too.

"Women quit strutting their stuff once they are comfortable with a man," Ken complained. "In the beginning, they keep their eyes on you while they're undressing, they walk toward you with that sexy walk. They play the game. Why does that have to end because two people are reasonably secure about each other's love?"

It doesn't. "The game"—visual arousal—can and should go on. And who knows how to play the game better than strippers, belly dancers, and exotic dancers, male and female? They practice the art of visual arousal, using eye contact and body movements to excite their audiences. They are consummate teases, promising something they won't deliver, yet leaving the paying customers happy though wanting more. I've interviewed a lot of men about sex—a thousand for *What Men Really Want*—and have frequently heard, "I wish my women would strip (or belly dance) for me."

That desire for a private erotic show is high on the male wish list under "more fellatio" and "more foreplay." (Surprised? Yes, they really do want more touching, kissing, caressing, fondling, and cuddling!) Stripping is an easily learned art. Even belly dancing isn't as difficult as you might think—particularly if you just borrow some of the moves to incorporate into a seductive walk or slow strip.

"The secret is in the eye contact," said Menaksha, a native of Pakistan who now resides in New York City.

Menaksha dances two nights a week at a Lebanese restaurant and several times a month at private dinners and parties. Her waistline is lithe, her belly slightly rounded but firm. And the hips are to die for, exactly round enough, without saddlebags or anything lumpy to distract the viewer when she's performing her sinewy dances.

"When I begin dancing, I don't focus on anyone in particular," she said. "This establishes the respect I want from the audience. Once I have that respect, I begin to flirt with my eyes, selecting certain men and looking into their eyes for several movements.

"And when I am dancing alone for my husband, I never take my eyes off him. As I dance, I let my eyes roam suggestively up and down his body, telegraphing my intentions for later. My eyes say things to him my lips are too shy to speak, even after twenty-two years of marriage."

She added, "I can't say enough that you must look into your lover's eyes while you are dancing or stripping exclusively for him. The effect of the dance as a prelude to lovemaking is diluted if you look off into the distance because you are too embarrassed about what you are doing. Take a class, or buy a book or video, and learn the basic moves. Practice them in front of a mirror while you look into your own eyes, pretending he is inside your reflection. But remember, the look is more important than swinging your hips."

I watched several belly dancers, strippers, and erotic dancers of both sexes in action, then interviewed them for suggestions on how ordinary men and women can incorporate erotic moves into their lovemaking.

The Pros' Top Five Visual Teases

- THE SLOW STRIP. The key is to keep your eyes locked onto your partner while slowly removing your clothes. Wear clothes that can be removed to good visual advantage. No dresses that must come off over the head, for example, or tight jeans. Blouses and shirts that can be unbuttoned to reveal sexy lingerie—or a hairy masculine chest—are good. No back-hook bras or plain old white underwear for either sex. Stockings rather than panty hose. "An ideal executive strip outfit," according to Cheryl, a former exotic dancer, "is a black skirt, black garter belt, very sheer black stockings, high heels, and a white silk shirt with white silk camisole underneath, no bra."

- THE PUBLIC STRIP. No, you don't actually remove all your clothes on the escalator at Bloomingdale's, only a piece here and there. In a restaurant, declare yourself "hot" and shrug gracefully out of your suit jacket, then unbutton one or two buttons to the top of your cleavage. Men, loosen your ties. And maintain eye contact the whole time. In a darkened theater, kick off a shoe, lean toward your partner, and run your foot across the top of his or hers.

• THE WET LOOK. Look at your partner from across the room and moisten your lips. Or meet him for dinner with a slicked-back hairstyle, something reminiscent of the after-shower look. Don't put up your umbrella in a fine mist. Dew on the skin is sexy, inviting, like the sweat of arousal. An exotic dancer told me she sprays a light mist of scented oil on her throat and chest before a date. In the candlelight, her chest gleams softly.

• THE PELVIC WALK. This loose, undulating sexy walk works whether you're moving briskly down a city street or slowly across the bedroom toward your lover. It looks like a toned-down version of the way models walk down runways. Some people have it naturally. Some women do it only when they wear high heels. You can get the walk down by practicing the following exercises to loosen the tightness in your pelvis. After a month of these exercises, you will have the fluid motion the walk requires. Once you have a loose pelvis, the walk is simple. Move from the hips in long, smooth strides.

The Pelvic Bounce. Lie on a bed or the floor on your back with palms on either side of your buttocks, knees bent. Lift your pelvis slightly and let it down, bouncing your lower back gently as you exhale sharply.

The Pelvic Thrust. Stand with your hands on your hips. Move your pelvic area in a circular motion to the right, then to the left. Exhale as you thrust your pelvis forward in the motion. Inhale on the backward pull. (Think of Brooke Shields as Rizzo with a hula hoop in the Broadway hit revival of *Grease.*)

The Yoga Cat Position. Get down on all fours. Inhale, letting your back sway. Bring your shoulders up and in. Lift up your head. Now exhale. Arch your upper back, tucking the pelvis in and under. Draw your diaphragm up and in and pull your anal muscles up and in. Bring your chin down toward your chest. Repeat ten times. Rest. Do another ten.

• HAND ON GENITALS. The women in the centerfold layouts are often photographed with hand on crotch, moist lips open, head thrown back, the pose suggestive of masturbation. And the men who dance in clubs for female audiences typically hold their crotches at least once or twice during a performance. A hand resting in the lap with fingers spread and pointing downward can make the same suggestion.

*T*HE PHYSICAL TEASE

The trouble with foreplay is its intent: to excite the partner sufficiently so that intercourse may be carried out. There is not enough play and almost no tease in foreplay, which is too forthright to be a good love game. We don't acknowledge the teasing phase even exists. The ancient Chinese, on the other hand, believed that playing at love added variety and excitement to erotic life. While they valued spontaneity, they also developed several games, enchanting in their whimsy and clever in their ability to arouse the creative spirit in lovers. The games are as delightful now as they were thousands of years ago.

Today the secrets of Chinese sexologists are taught largely by former monks to a very small and select group of Western clients.

"There will be no exchange of bodily fluids and no penetration, not even what you Americans call 'the foreplay,'" Ragapanu had assured me. "But you will have the erotic experience of your life. Shall I put you down in my book for next Saturday?"

In the interests of research, I agreed to spend a day with Raga-panu, a sex guru from Nepal, who travels twice a year to the States to work with clients, wealthy married couples in Manhattan and Los Angeles who pay him to teach them new sexual tricks or show them, hands on, how to put the sizzle back into their erotic lives. On a mild January day, I met Ragapanu at his suite—courtesy of a client—at the exclusive and discreet Mark Hotel on the Upper East Side of Manhattan. I was not expecting the erotic experience of my life, a designation I typically award to something that has occurred within the past month or two. Penetration is definitely required for that accolade.

"I will do nothing but teach you how to tease," he said after we'd exchanged greetings and bowed from the waist to each other.

He was slight and wizened in appearance, his dark brown skin looking more like the result of too many hours in the California sun than heredity. It was difficult to guess his age—somewhere between thirty and fifty?—and he would not tell. The cloying scent of floral incense filled the suite, which was beautifully decorated with fine cherry furniture. He handed me a soft white terry sheet and sent me into the bathroom to remove any clothing and bathe.

"Am I to return wearing nothing but this?" I asked, indicating the sheet.

"Yes, but yes," he said, nodding politely, bowing from the waist again.

After I had bathed and creamed my body, he showed me the Chinese brush pen that he planned to use first and instructed me to lie "nude and passive" on the king-size bed with my eyes closed. The brush made of black fox hair set in a bamboo tube had a deli-cate point. Not trusting myself to keep my eyes closed, I asked to wear the black satin blindfold I saw on the night table. He consented.

"This brush is the spring butterfly," he said. "You are the field of flowers. Imagine the butterfly flitting rapidly from one flower to the next. One does not know where the butterfly will land or how long it will stay before flitting to the next flower. Later I will show you how to vary the pressure when you touch. For now, I want you to feel and not think about how it is happening."

And later, he would tell me he carefully selected the spots on my body known by the ancient Chinese as the "pleasure points," but at the time I thought his ministrations were random. I felt the butterfly, the tip of the brush, land on the arch of my right foot and move quickly from there to the left arch and between the toes, then kissing the tips of my toes. The feeling of the brush on my feet was akin to a moving tickle, and it made me smile. Suddenly the butterfly took off in bursts of flight, barely stopping to touch my ankles, calves, knees. The skin on my inner thighs was tingling, expecting the kiss, when the quixotic butterfly landed again between my toes, his touch more firm this time.

The butterfly lingered on the soles of my feet, darted to my armpits, and settled delicately on my nipple. In my mind's eye I could see it, an enormous and brilliantly colored monarch, resting on my nipple. The sun was shining and my skin grew hot basking in the rays.

"Uhm," I said, arching my back, upsetting the butterfly who took off and landed this time in my groin.

In his wake, the butterfly left my skin tingling. Faster he fluttered, landing so quickly and softly sometimes I barely knew he was there until he'd moved on to the next place. Abruptly, the butterfly stopped. Regretfully, I pictured him flying off to another field.

"I am dipping the end of the brush in an aromatic oil," Ragapanu said. "The sensations will be much different now."

Yes, the butterfly was gone, replaced by an oiled brush, a sleek ravenous animal that went round and round my nipples until they were standing erect. The hands at my sides stirred.

"I want to touch myself," I told him, slightly breathless.

"Keep your hands at your sides," he insisted, moving the brush quickly between my breasts.

Ragapanu opened my legs, which I had squeezed together, and used the brush to flirt with my perineum and vulva. It ran up and down my private parts, and I felt myself grow wet. Then Ragapanu brushed my clitoris, first in upward strokes, next in a circling motion. When he stopped, I flexed my muscles, attempting to pull the brush inside to the place where I wanted it, my clitoris. He followed my lead and stroked my clitoris again until I was moving in time with him. Without warning, he stopped, leaving me panting and on the verge of begging this little man—whom I hadn't found the least bit attractive before I put on the blindfold and he picked up the brush—to fuck me, *please.*

"I am going to touch you with a feather now," he said.

My hands clutched the sheets in frustration. A feather?

Ah, but the feather surprised me.

He ran it—a peacock feather, I later saw—along the sides of my breasts, then between them, creating cooling shivers up and down my spine. The feather glided down my body, playing from belly to groin, causing some of the heat on my skin to dissipate. With his hands, he parted my vulva and used the feather to tease my clitoris, bringing it to full attention again. I gasped with pleasure.

Like a virtuoso, Ragapanu played my clitoris, using his feather to pull an orgasm that spilled from my body in corkscrew spirals, the spasms following the path of a twirling feather.

"I meant only to tease you," he said, whether an apology for exceeding the bounds of the lesson or a disclaimer made from false modesty, I do not know.

It was my turn to pick up the brush.

I went to an Oriental stationery store to purchase a brush pen to teach my lover the game. The store clerk did not immediately know what I was talking about. Finally, it dawned on her.

"A calligraphy pen," she said, and then I remembered that Ragapanu told me this game had been invented by a Chinese calligrapher.

If you cannot find a brush pen, or calligraphy pen, an artist's brush will do. Avoid ones with flat, square, or stiff bristles. Soft sable-haired round brushes are the best.

A friend who tried the butterfly tease with an artist's sable brush reported: "My girlfriend said I had never turned her on as much as I did with that brush. She made my body sing, too. We were both amazed at the erotic power of that tiny little tool. I am buying them by the dozen now."

And another friend reported, "The butterfly tease heightened the sexual feelings for both of us. We were tingling with desire when we started making love. My boyfriend said his skin had never felt so sensitive to touch."

She added, "Using the blindfold is a good idea. If you are the one being teased, you are more aroused by not knowing where the brush will land. It's like all your skin stands at attention waiting for the touch. And if you are the one performing the tease, you may want to peek at the instructions below to be sure you're hitting the points—and you don't want your partner to see you do that. It would take the feeling of spontaneity entirely out of the game."

Variations on the Game

• *THE FEATHER TEASE.* According to Ragapanu, the feather tease was invented centuries ago in China by noblemen during a period when the peacock feather was a decoration awarded to those who had served the emperor well. Any feather—peacock, ostrich, even chicken—can be used in the same way the Chinese brush pen is used.

A friend who has incorporated the teases into her lovemaking shared one of her own feather games. She said, "I have a collection of feather masks, many from Mardi Gras, with elaborate and dripping feathers. In my own variation of the feather tease, I wear a mask while performing fellatio on my partner. The feathers tickle and caress the base of his penis, his scrotum, and groin while I have him in my mouth. Sometimes I manipulate the feathers only. Drives men wild!"

• SPIDER'S LEGS—OR, PATTES D'ARAIGNÉE. In this French version of the Chinese butterfly, use the fingertips and finger pads to play lightly over your partner's body hair and skin. Long fingernails will have to be trimmed if you're going to use the tips effectively.

• THE SCENT KISS. Perfume only the parts of your body you want your lover to touch. This may be the obvious places, such as genitals, or those places you secretly wish she or he would pay more attention to, like armpits, the backs of knees, inside the elbows. Have him or her sniff lightly to find the scent and then inhale deeply only those perfumed spots. No touching. He is kissing you with his nose. Be sure he likes the scent before you do this. This is no time to try a new perfume.

• SILK TEASE. Use only a silk scarf, not a synthetic substitute. Crumple the fabric in your hands. Then use it to caress parts of your lover's body.

Pleasure Points

According to ancient Chinese erotic texts, each of us, male and female, has certain "acupoints," spots that when stimulated cause immediate sexual arousal, boost sexual stamina, and recharge the autonomic nervous system controlling many sexual sensations and functions. Whether or not erotic stimuli applied to these acupoints can actually boost and recharge may depend on one's ability to believe they do. But tickling the spots will result in an immediate pleasurable experience.

The major pleasure points are, not surprisingly, located on the torso.

They include:

• THE MIDPOINT OF THE PERINEUM, located between the base of the scrotum and the anus in men and the vaginal opening and the anus in women. Experiment until you find the spot on your partner's perineum, which, when pressed lightly, causes pleasurable sensations. Consider this the midpoint.

• *THE CINNABAR FIELD*.   A line of seven points from the navel to the pubic symphysis, at the front of the pubic bone, above the genitals. Imagine a line connecting the navel and the pubic symphysis, with five additional points each spaced more or less equidistant from the others. Press each for three to five seconds, then press again.

• *NIPPLES*.   Both male and female.

• *BREASTS*.   On each breastbone, approximately nipple level. There are two more points at the midpoints of the base of the breasts.

• *GROIN*.   A pair of pleasure points are located somewhere along the crease between the abdomen and the thighs.

*T*EASING WITH A PENIS

Men adore our breasts. For many of them, making love to breasts ideally includes intramammary intercourse, or lovemaking *à l'espagnol*. (In the days before reliable birth control, Spanish men attempted to persuade their women this was a safe and satisfying form of substitute intercourse.)

A man holds the woman's breasts together around his penis and gently thrusts. The sensations are exciting for both of them.

"I have very sensitive breasts," one woman said, "and have been orgasmic this way. I also enjoy feeling my husband ejaculate on my breasts. It's a special way of making love once in a while."

Armpits, buttocks, and inner thighs can also be used as alternate areas for intercourse. In some societies, such forms of intercourse were sanctioned as ways of preventing unwanted pregnancy. The Zulu warriors, for example, were permitted to move their penises between the thighs of virgins. The practice was called "wiping of the spears."

Modern lovers can play teasing games by moving the penis against breasts, buttocks, and other body parts.

Part 2

AND THEN AGAIN,
IT'S IN YOUR HANDS

Chapter Four

MASTURBATION, HERS

*T*he room was redolent of the warm, musky scent of perfumed women sweating. Their soft sighs and moans, stifled groans, and animal grunts surrounded me in a distaff symphony of sexual noises. Legs open, heads thrown back, their intimate parts largely hidden by their whirring vibrators, they masturbated to orgasm.

After they caught their collective breath, the women "shared" their feelings with workshop leader Betty Dodson.

"This was fun!" said a buxom regional magazine editor. "It blew my mind. As a little girl, I never got to be part of a circle jerk. Girls didn't get to jerk off in circles. Little boys bonded through showing off their penises. Why can't girls bond the same way? This completes something for me."

"I never knew what other women really look like when they come," said a community college teacher. "I've seen women have orgasms in the movies, but I always suspected their performances were exaggerated. Now I know I was right. Orgasm doesn't look like a grand mal seizure for real women. I feel okay about myself and the way I come now. I can stop comparing myself to a gloriously writhing myth."

A woman who thinks she was an Egyptian princess in another

life said, "This is a healing experience for me. I've only been able to have orgasms when masturbating and never with a partner, even if he takes a lot of time to stimulate me orally and manually. I think I'll be able to have an orgasm with a partner now because of this workshop. The fear I had about letting go in front of someone is gone."

And a businesswoman in her early thirties discovered she'd been having "little orgasms" without knowing she had. "Maybe now," she said, "they will grow bigger. I will be able to have bigger orgasms in my life."

"I had sex with a partner before I masturbated," said a recently divorced nurse in her thirties. "Most men have masturbated for years before they have sex with a woman. We are at a disadvantage. They know their own genitals. We don't. At last I am getting acquainted with my genitals and learning what they are capable of doing for me."

When it was my turn to comment, I'm embarrassed to admit I mumbled something about how liberating it was to masturbate in public. I did not have an orgasm, but I lied and said I did. Yes, I faked an orgasm in the orgasm workshop, which guarantees no one leaves without coming. Why lie? Ego. Professional courtesy. Embarrassment. Fear? Maybe Betty would have made me stay until I really did have an orgasm. Maybe she would have made me stay until everyone else had gone home and then made me watch her play with Clitty Ann.

I lied to get out of there, which is much the same reason women often lie in bed: to end the sex. Though I often wish I could be, I'm not a group person. I can only come in the company of one lover— or perhaps a guru devoting himself to my personal instruction. Faced with more than two people assembled for the purpose of exploring and exposing, I hide behind a mask, admiring the people who can truly utilize such group dynamics to improve their personal lives. I take my notes away with me, like the proverbial squirrel hoarding the nuts, pour over them at home, and savor the information alone. I am and always have been self-taught. Many of you, I suspect, are like me in this regard.

The other women in Betty's workshop got something out of the experience, something beyond their orgasm. They got permission to have more orgasms, either with lovers or alone.

"I'm going to make a date with myself next weekend," the editor said as we were leaving together.

Betty Dodson makes masturbation dates with herself. She enters "self-loving" into her datebook and allows at least an hour. Personally, I would rather be spontaneous with myself. But if you need permission to masturbate—as many women do—Betty is the goddess of self-love.

THE BETTY DODSON TRAINING

A slightly overweight woman in her early sixties, Betty when dressed looks no more like "The Mother of Masturbation" than a million other women who might accidentally bump into you with their shopping carts in the fresh produce section. She will not be dressed if you meet her for the first time at one of her workshops, where she answers the door in the nude. Her masturbation workshops, called Bodysex Groups, grew out of her experience with women in CR (consciousness raising) groups of the seventies. Many of these women, she learned, had never had orgasms. They were waiting for love to transport them to the state of ecstasy and it never did.

"The economic value of female genitalia affected our sexuality," she explains. "Whether we are saving sex for our prince, bestowing sex freely on our lover, or granting exclusive rights in marriage, we are doing business with sex. As long as women do not have economic parity, we will be unconsciously bargaining with sex for economic support. Women are sexually repressed because we are economically dependent."

Betty told women to deal with their repression by taking their vibrators into their own hands. Yet she is not a stereotypical male-bashing angry woman. In an early exercise, women pretended to be men. For three minutes by the egg timer, women assumed the missionary position, putting all their weight on their arms, and pumped their hips furiously over imaginary lovers as Betty exhorted, "Keep your arms straight! Don't crush your lover! You're too high up! Your penis just fell out! Don't stop moving or you'll lose your erection! Don't move too fast or you'll come too soon! And don't forget to whisper sweet nothings in her ear!"

"It was hysterically funny—and enlightening," said a woman who had attended one of those sessions. "At the end of three minutes, we were panting and exhausted and asking, 'How do men do this, anyway?' It gave us empathy for men."

At the beginning of the session I attended, eleven naked women sat in a circle examining their genitals with oversized handheld mirrors. Well, they were naked except for the earrings almost everyone wore and the occasional watch, bracelet, or necklace in the form of an amulet. They ranged in age from twenty-six to fifty-four and worked in various fields, including publishing, business, teaching, and nursing. Some had children and one had grandchildren. Two lesbians, one bisexual, and eight heterosexuals—they were slim to medium in build, small to medium breasted, with the exception of a forty-three-year-old, who described herself accurately as "frankly fat." ("Real bodies," Betty enthused. "Let go of those idealized media images of female bodies and love yourself.") They were all white women. No one had long hair. I don't know why this puzzled me, but it did.

Some women, however, had a lot more pubic hair than an acquaintance with men's magazines and X-rated videos had led me to believe existed in nature. Pubic hair curling in thick patches of springy tendrils that must poke through the crotches of panties, pubic hair spreading onto their inner thighs, pubic hair that, yes, looks long enough to braid. I was fascinated by the variety of pubic hair.

"Masturbation is a primary form of sexual expression," Betty told us. "It's not just for kids or for when you're in between lovers or when you end up alone in old age. Masturbation is the ongoing love affair that each of us has with ourselves throughout our lifetime."

If you resent your mother for not teaching you to masturbate, you'll love Betty Dodson.

"It's show-and-tell time," she told the class as she parted her labia to expose the hood of her clitoris. "Meet Clitty Ann." She pulled the hood back in a dramatic introduction of her own clitoris. "Isn't she beautiful?"

Everybody shows and tells in Betty's workshops. She considers this a necessary part of self-love. The inevitable flower comparisons were made as we parted the moist folds to display the buds. We saw that some lips are thick and pendulous and some lips are thin, delicate rather than lush, and some clitorises are large and protruding, while others are tiny nubs well hidden by their hoods. Yes, everyone looks different and somehow the same once the curtains of pubic hair have been parted.

After show-and-tell, we blew our noses. We oiled a finger and penetrated each nostril. (No, I don't quite understand why . . . something about opening ourselves up to pleasure.) We breathed deep breaths followed by fire breaths (see page 17). Finally, we assumed the goddess position (flat on our backs, knees bent, bottoms of feet touching so that our legs were folded into diamond shapes) and started our motors—*vibrators*—racing. Before an easily orgasmic woman could launch into orbit, Betty ordered the vibrators turned off again. It was time to talk about our genital memories and sexual feelings. I was unfairly annoyed with the process. If you accept that many women have let societal prohibitions keep them from masturbating, then must you not also accept that they will need a great deal of verbal encouragement to freely indulge in masturbating?

But genital memories?

The first time I touched myself, my mother yelled at me. And, I didn't look like my brother. Or, I was ashamed of what was between my legs. I don't know where the shame came from. Maybe it was instinctive. Those genital memories.

Sex is meditation, an opening for me to connect with my higher self. Sex is spirituality; spirituality is sex. My body is always there for me. Those sexual feelings. *This is the first time I haven't felt ashamed of wanting to caress my own little pink rosebud; now I know it's okay to love her, to want to be with her alone sometimes.*

When women talk about sex, they talk about their relationships, even if the relationships are with themselves. Have we been so conditioned to connect our sexual feelings to some entity greater than our body parts that we can't even simplify masturbation? Yes, in many cases, we have.

"We will all be better lovers when we can love ourselves better," Betty said.

I had thought we were going to get in touch with our clitorises, not our spirits. And I had expected a hands-on experience, not this exercise in battery power. Why were we touching ourselves with vibrators, not fingers? Does Mommy not want us touching ourselves after all? ("Most women can have an orgasm using a vibrator," Betty explained later. "If they don't have orgasms easily, they may need the extra stimulation of the vibrator. And if they aren't comfortable touching themselves, they will feel less threatened by touching themselves with a vibrator.")

"When everyone grows up with positive images of their cunts, no one will secretly think of herself as genitally deformed," Betty said.

We shared more feelings. There was much talk about sweat, body smells—all of which we embrace!—periods, stretch marks, the scars from episiotomies, and PC muscles.

"Just the other day I saw a bright pink button that said, *'Viva la Vulva!'*" Betty said.

We changed positions—to anything other than the positions we were in, possibly to keep the joints from locking—and started the engines again. Before she could stop us this time, some of us came and, yes, at least one of us faked. Vibrator orgasms are quicker and frequently less intense than manual orgasms. I wasn't missing anything anyway, I rationalized. Was I grumpy because I don't seem to be able to have an orgasm in a group setting?

My experience with Betty's workshop was not the universal one. The other participants called the session "empowering," "remarkable," "liberating," "a celebration of the sacred joys of masturbation." These women got permission to enjoy their sexuality independent of their partners and support for the feelings of warmth toward other women, feelings that may be new to them. A forty-five-year-old divorced mother told me she had never been given support for her sexuality by other women until she attended this workshop. Betty focuses not on the techniques of self-pleasuring, but on the politics of masturbation, on "liberating masturbation" from the control of the male patriarchy—whatever that means—and, more important, on telling women it really is okay to love yourself.

"Little boys are encouraged to be penis proud," one woman said. "Little girls are not allowed to be vulva proud. Maybe some of us need that encouragement no matter how old we are to move beyond being little girls in the bedroom."

If you need permission to masturbate and/or reinforcement in your belief that female genitalia is beautiful, buy Betty Dodson's book or video, both titled *Sex for One,* which I also highly recommend for the bi-curious. Betty is open about her own "bisexual feminism," her perspective on sexuality. If you have not explored that part of yourself and want to do so, you will find this a comfortable place to begin.

The video, which is long on theory and short on directions, tells you to love yourself in the following manner.

The Dodson Path to Glory

• Blow your nose. Dip a finger in oil and penetrate each nostril. (You are clearing your breathing passages.)

• Breathe deeply until you are relaxed. Follow with fire-breathing until you feel erotically energized. (See techniques for deep breathing and fire-breathing on pages 16–17.)

• Assume the goddess pose: flat on your back, knees bent, bottoms of feet touching so that your legs are folded into a diamond shape. Turn on your vibrator. (See vibrator techniques, page 230.)

• Assume the rear-entry position. Prop the vibrator on a pillow and hump it.

• Lie on your back. Pump up your buttocks muscles when you feel orgasm is imminent.

• Assume the goddess pose, breathe, and reflect.

MASTURBATION IS A LEARNING EXPERIENCE

"I didn't know how to ask my partner to touch me until I began masturbating at age thirty," said Cassidy, who celebrated her fortieth birthday by buying herself a deluxe vibrator with attachments. "I went through my twenties depending on men to know how to satisfy me and being angry and disappointed when they didn't. I wasted a lot of good years and wrongly blamed a few good men."

Cassidy and I were talking about masturbation at the Good Vibrations store for sex toys, books, and videos in San Francisco—the store where she had bought her birthday vibrator. The staff at Good Vibrations is enthusiastic about masturbation. There is no better place in the country to have this discussion.

"We think masturbation should be the national pastime," the sales clerk, a cheerful and attractive middle-aged lesbian, said. "It feels good, it's healthy, it's natural, it's free, it's legal, it's your birthright, it's easy to do, it's convenient, it's voluntary, you can do it alone, you can do it with a partner, it's relaxing . . ."

I suspected she'd memorized the litany, but she said it with feeling anyway.

The shop is not large but has an impressive array of products tastefully displayed, a large mail-order catalog business, and a staff that is equally comfortable with gay, lesbian, and heterosexual customers. There is something for everyone here, and no one is made to feel unwelcome or out of place. Periodically they hold classes on how to use vibrators and other equipment and also give instruction (using plastic models, not the real thing) on masturbation techniques. And I like the fact that they call it *masturbation,* not "self-loving" or "solo sex" or "autoeroticism" or any of those words that, to me at least, seem designed to disguise the fact that you're touching your own genitals as if there were something wrong with doing it.

"They taught me how to masturbate," Cassidy said. "I am embarrassed to admit I had to be taught, but I did."

Cassidy need not be embarrassed. Images of women masturbating may be staples of erotic art, but the pleasure-phobic Puritans, our founding ancestors, left us a legacy of guilt about masturbation. They inherited the grief from their own ancestors. The word *masturbate* comes from the Latin *manu stuprare,* meaning "to defile oneself with one's hand." The taboo against masturbation has its roots in the religious dictates against any sexual activity that is not procreative. (Only the Greeks thought masturbation was a laudable practice.) The Victorians called the practice "self-abuse." So pervasive was the stigma attached to self-stimulation that the American Medical Association did not declare masturbation a "normal" sexual activity until 1972!

Women have traditionally been more likely than men to take the prohibitions against touching ourselves to heart. One obvious reason: The male genitalia is on the outside of the body, where it is hard to ignore or resist, while the female genitalia is hidden, requiring us to search actively for it and thus consciously break the rule. Also, little girls are raised on the fairy tales that promise the prince will kiss them and ignite their passion. (The male gives pleasure; the female doesn't take it for herself.) Boys grow up believing they must assume the active role. Social conditioning has reinforced female sexual passivity. Nature and nurture have conspired to keep women the masturbation-impaired gender.

"I didn't touch myself," Cassidy said. "My body was a mystery to me until I was past thirty, when I finally began to learn about myself and sex."

At her Good Vibrations training session, she and a half-dozen other women were taught to use their newly purchased vibrators and given suggestions for manual masturbation as well.

"After the store closed at seven, they set up some folding chairs in a circle around a table filled with demonstrator products," she said. "We were all wearing business suits and looked like a group of women who were about to be described as 'formerly uptight.' The instructors were great. They used their hands as vaginas and also had a vulva puppet. There was laughter as they showed us how not to put the vibrator right on the clitoris and things like that. It was a very relaxed atmosphere.

"They showed us the basic hand position for manual masturbation—two fingers pointing in a downward V surrounding the clitoris, so that pressure is applied to the sides and top. This may sound crazy, but I didn't know that was how you did it until they showed us."

For most of us, masturbation is the first sexual self-learning experience—even if it comes late—and the basis for good sex throughout our lives. We need not stop learning when we become sexually active with partners. What we learn alone with ourselves can be shared with our partners to make lovemaking better for everyone.

While men tend to take penis in hand and pump in a fast up-and-down motion, women masturbate in a variety of ways.

"I use the flat of my hand to grind my clitoris while I insert my fingers into my vagina," one woman said.

"I twist my clitoris between my index finger and thumb," said another, describing a technique that would be too rough for most women to enjoy.

Other women lie on their backs, holding their legs tightly together as they press against the vulva—or use the spray of a shower jet to stimulate the clitoris—or use pillows, towels, or blankets to rub the clitoris.

The following directions are synthesized from the advice of women who freely and joyously masturbate, the staff of Good Vibrations, and the sex therapist and author of *For Yourself,* Lonnie Barbach, Ph.D.

The Private Lesson

• Close your eyes and relax. Breathe deeply and rhythmically. Imagine that you are feeling pleasure in each part of your body, one part at a time, beginning with your toes. Feel that pleasure moving like warm fingers from one place to another.

• Warm body lotion or oil by placing the bottle in hot water. Stroke yourself all over with the warmed oil or lotion. Focus your attention on how your hands feel on each part of your body.

• Massage and touch yourself all over in different ways, using some of the techniques from the teasing games on page 49. Note what touch pleases and what arouses.

• Now use those arousing touches on your breasts, belly, thighs. Again, pay attention to what arouses you quickly and more slowly. When you know your paths to orgasm, you can share them with your lover by guiding his hands.

• Stroke your labia lips lightly. Insert a finger into your vagina.

• Run your finger along the clitoris and up over the shaft. Massage the clitoris lightly between two fingers. Then try a circular motion. Vary your strokes and rhythms. Feel the orgasm in your fingertips.

- To learn how intense a delayed orgasm can be, experiment with masturbation interruptus. Get yourself highly aroused, then stop. Repeat, repeat, repeat.

THE FANTASY CONNECTION

For some, masturbation is the safe place to explore fantasies we can't or won't share with partners, fantasies about activities we have no desire to pursue in real life. It is the thought of them, not the acting out, that arouses. Therapists generally say that fantasies about rape, sadomasochism, group sex, and other taboo subjects are common and harmless—unless they become compulsive and obsessive. You can explore dangerous territory while masturbating without suffering any ill effects. Nor should you feel the need to "share" those fantasies with your partner. In fact, sharing our deepest fantasies can rob them of their arousal power.

Past sexual experiences often provide the scripts for self-arousal. Or you can use masturbatory fantasies as dress rehearsals for erotic encounters you want to have. Consider erotic fantasies your own private bijou of the mind. You can play any film you want, whenever you want, as often as you want.

"I had a standard fantasy for years," Cathy said. "I was the bride having sex in my wedding gown. Now I am much more creative."

"Two or three times a month I indulge in S&M fantasies," Carol said. "I bought a studded slave collar and wrist bands to wear when I do. I pinch my nipples and pretend I'm wearing nipple clamps."

Jennie indulges her S&M fantasies while masturbating, too—but she puts herself in the dominant position.

"I like to dress for the occasion, in high heels and black stockings and bustier," she said. "I might use my belt to whack the pillow and pretend it's a tasty male ass. I get off on playing dom—but I would die before I'd let my boyfriend see me like that!"

Some women masturbate to flowery romantic fantasies. Others

imagine they are making love to men they cannot have, like their sister's husband or their husband's best friend or Tom Cruise. No matter what the story line, for women the fantasy is a key element of masturbation. Many men masturbate to images of body parts, not stories. Few women do.

"I can't masturbate without a script," Cheryl said. "I can get aroused by playing with myself, but I can't get aroused enough to come unless I am following a story in my head."

Mutual Masturbation

I've interviewed many women who've told me that they never masturbate. For my book *Sexual Pleasures,* I talked to over eight hundred women and almost twenty percent said they had never masturbated—and some said it proudly as if masturbation was a sin or a sign of weakness. For those women and for others who want to practice safe sex with a new partner or for any woman who would like to turn her man on in a special way, mutual masturbation is the answer.

Many women initially find the idea of masturbating in front of their partner unappealing or intimidating. Maybe they think masturbation "should" be private, or that couples "shouldn't" masturbate at all. But many men fantasize about having a woman masturbate for them.

"I thought I would look funny," Josie said. "I thought I wouldn't be able to have an orgasm because I'd be too self-conscious. But I got over that when he started masturbating. He excited me. I wanted to excite him. I got into it."

"It allows me to explore my body at my own pace while I am being stimulated by my lover's presence," said Kelly. "And it's a wonderful opportunity to show a new man how you come. Everyone learns something from mutual masturbation."

The Technique

• Set the mood, just as you would for solo masturbation or for any other romantic form of couple sex. Use soft lighting.

• Take a shower or bath together or stroke and caress each other as if you were going to make love.

• If you don't want to be nude, wear minimal sexy clothing that will permit your partner a good view—for example, a negligee and nothing else.

• Take your time. Describe what you are doing and how it feels as you're stroking yourself.

• The man should vary stroking the penis with fondling his balls or caressing his body—to delay ejaculation. He may need to stop periodically or apply very minimal pressure to sustain an erection without ejaculating.

• Ask questions, such as "How strong are you gripping your penis?" "How hard are you pressing against your clitoris?"

• As a variation, you each should masturbate with your eyes closed and let your other senses—smell, sound, hearing—arouse you. Or masturbate in each other's arms. Or masturbate yourself while he kisses and caresses you and vice versa. Or use mutual masturbation as foreplay.

• Afterward, hold each other.

A friend who had not tried mutual masturbation until recently said: "This is such an intimate way to make love. I thought it would be cold or clinical, but it isn't at all. There is something very special about opening yourself up to a partner this way—and having him be equally open to you. This is sharing a very secret part of you. I was very aroused and also very moved by the experience."

Chapter Five

MASTURBATION, HIS

*M*y housekeeper left a feather duster behind last week and I didn't take a minute to see the possibilities in it," said Josh, who is sharing his masturbation story with a group of men in his Erotic Body Workshop. "I put on a cock ring and, when my dick was hard, dusted it all over. Then I laid back, put the feather duster over my dick, and began thrusting faster and faster against the soft and slippery feathers.

"I stopped myself before I made a mess of those beautiful feathers."

This is not your mother's masturbation workshop I was watching on videotape. No paeans to the metallic scent of menstrual blood. No mirrors necessary to view the hidden treasure. There was no show-and-tell. What's to show that's not been showing all along? The penis is many things, but not a mystery. When men talk about masturbation, they describe how they stroked and how hard and how high they came and how it felt.

A workshop for male masturbation? You know the old joke: Ninety-nine out of one hundred men masturbate and the other guy lies. Long before masturbation was deemed "normal," some famous men admitted to doing it—Rousseau, Goethe, Kierkegaard, among them. Why do men need instruction in doing the obvious thing?

"I'm all I have for a while, so I want to make the best of myself," said Josh, a gay man in his late thirties, who has chosen "the path of creative celibacy" because he is afraid of contracting the AIDS virus.

The giggle elicited by his feather duster story died in my throat. There is nothing wrong with finding humor in sex. Would that more people could laugh and play in bed! And laughing about sex is a good way for people to release their embarrassment about their own and others' sexual feelings. But, for many gay men, masturbation, including mutual masturbation, has replaced sex outside the confines of a committed monogamous relationship. There is even a store devoted solely to masturbation in San Francisco's Castro district, home to the largest concentration of gay men in America. The AutoErotic stocks lubricants and anal vibrators, videos and books on masturbation, and other aides for men to use alone or in mutual masturbation with a partner.

The workshop was not limited to gay men. Heterosexual men had their own reasons for being there.

"Men need something like this to put us back in touch with our bodies," said Paul, a thirty-nine-year-old heterosexual divorced man. "Social conditioning teaches men to disconnect with our bodies. We learned to make love by desensitizing ourselves. I remember buying a tube of desensitizing cream to rub on my penis so I could last longer in bed—when I was in high school. It didn't work. It would take a lot of desensitizing to shut down a seventeen-year-old kid's cock.

"But I did learn how to last longer by taking my mind off fucking while I was fucking. I want to unlearn that technique. I want to enjoy every stroke—and still last longer. I want to be the kind of lover women want and I want to enjoy myself, too. That's why I'm here."

Alan was looking for the way to unite his heart, genitals, and soul. Matt wanted to learn techniques to enhance his sexual pleasure and that of his partner. Jeff was there because his wife "is into New

Age stuff." She promised to forgo their joint vacation so he could attend a camp for amateur athletes run by retired pro ballplayers if he would take the Body Erotic workshop and accompany her on a couples tantric sex retreat weekend.

"She's getting the better end of the deal," he said, grimacing after Lance, twenty-one and gay, told of how aroused he'd become when he'd discovered a jar of lubricant left behind by a visiting object of lust—so aroused, he'd used the entire contents on a marathon masturbatory session.

"I come too fast," one man said. "I'm here because I heard about all the different strokes that make masturbation last longer. If I can master the strokes, maybe I can make intercourse last longer."

"I lose my erections sometimes," a middle-aged man said. "I want to learn how to keep the erection going strong."

"I want to come more than once because my wife would love for me to be able to do that," a young man said, looking straight into the camera, touching in his vulnerability. "I want to be a better lover for her."

If only women saw men this way, vulnerable, wanting to please, fearing sexual failure. Women worry about having orgasms or having bigger and better ones. Men worry about "giving" women pleasure. The quality of their own orgasms is less important to them than making sure she has orgasms.

I fast-forwarded the tape. The fourteen men were standing in the circle, and their hands held penises sheathed in shiny condoms. Long, sensuous strokes, milking strokes, delicate strokes, double-handed strokes, rapid up-and-down strokes blended together in something that should have been set to music. Some held their testicles with one hand and masturbated with the other.

"Okay, stop," said a voice from outside the circle.

The men stopped. The delay was part of the learning process, meant to teach them to delay gratification. In this circle on hold, there was no talk of genital memories, but of balls and nipples.

I like to have mine fondled, rubbed, and tugged away from my body be-

fore I come. I want her to suck them before she gives me head, but I don't want her to touch them while we're fucking. I don't like my nipples fondled. It turns me on to have my nipples kissed and sucked and bitten.

They started again. Gentlemen, rev your engines, I was thinking.

"I want you to use the vibrator for at least five minutes," the instructor said.

They vibrated and stroked, stopped, and started again, and finally began to come in a series of yelps and moans, one after another, like a popcorn popper full of kernels heated to the explosion point. Inside the safety jackets of their condoms, the penises shivered, then shriveled. It was a circle jerk without the mess.

"What an experience," Josh of the feather duster said. "It was erotic and spiritual at the same time."

Jeff, who had complained about attending the workshop to please his wife, nodded his head vigorously in agreement. Who would have thought?

*T*HE BODY ELECTRIC PHILOSOPHY

Chinese Taoist practices were based on the belief that female energy, yin, was inexhaustible, while male energy, yang, was in limited supply and must be conserved. Women were encouraged to have orgasms through masturbation and lovemaking. Men were taught to make love without ejaculating as often as possible.

Taking that line of reasoning ever further, in 1758, S. A. Tissot, a Swiss doctor, published *Onanism: Treatise on the Diseases Produced by Masturbation,* the classic tract on masturbation that influenced popular thinking for more than a hundred years. We owe to him the belief that semen lost during masturbation was equivalent to the loss of blood, leaving the masturbator weakened and susceptible to any number of diseases. Tissot also believed that a man could become insane from excessive masturbation—and that a man could even masturbate himself to death. Have the sex-addiction theorists borrowed anything from the Swiss doctor?

The promoted "cures" for masturbation have included everything from bondage belts, penis rings, and restraints to a course of cold baths, fresh air, and bland food. John Kellogg invented his breakfast flakes as part of the anti-masturbation regime offered to patients in his Battle Creek Sanitarium, the nineteenth century's version of a health spa. How thinking has changed—all the way back to the ancient Chinese, with a new twist. Delaying ejaculation to prolong pleasure is the goal. And masturbation is part of the cure.

"In contrast to the ancient Chinese concept of sex as energy—*ching chi,* a life force that can take you to high erotic states and keep you there for hours—most Western men's erotic experience is balloon sex: You tense your legs, squeeze your chest, and blow up the middle till it pops," said Joseph Kramer, who founded the Body Electric School in Oakland, California, in 1984.

The school offers workshops on techniques based on Tantric and Taoist traditions and Native American rituals (most notably shamanic drumming) for men and women and couples in several U.S. cities, Canada, and Europe. It is licensed by the state of California to train masseurs, and sponsors weeklong retreats in California, New England, the Catskill Mountains, Key West, and other places.

"Most Western sex is necrophilia, one dead body having sex with another dead body," according to Kramer.

In the workshops for men, participants learn how to perform erotic massage and to extend arousal and intensify orgasmic pleasure. There are, he claims, "twenty strokes other than basic up-and-down-the-shaft-till-he-squirts." The orgasmically adept can also achieve a whole-body orgasm through Kramer's techniques. Born and raised in a devout Catholic St. Louis family, Kramer, who left a Jesuit seminary to find his sexual identity, has studied under Native American and Eastern erotic masters and is one of a growing number of American teacher/practitioners, mostly in major East and West Coast cities.

What made him develop a masturbation workshop for men?

"I loved to masturbate from the first time I grabbed my little penis when I was five years old. As I got older, I realized there should

be more to the experience for adults and I had to look outside Western sex traditions to find that. My quest made me realize that men
have so much to learn about sexual pleasuring, both of themselves
and their partners, and that they probably won't learn it from sources
within the Western traditions."

The Multi-Stroke Technique

• Rub a small amount of lubricant, or saliva if you prefer,
in the palms of your hands and into your fingertips. Use the
following strokes in various combinations. When you feel
close to ejaculation, switch strokes and vary pressure and
speed. After a while, you will be able to masturbate for
longer periods of time without ejaculating.

• *THE DOUBLE-RING STRETCH STROKE.*   Good for
coaxing a half-erect penis to full erection. Make a ring with
the thumb and index finger of each hand. Place one above
the other on the shaft of the penis around the base. Use firm
pressure. Holding one ring around the base, move the other
up toward the head of the penis, stretching the penis as you
move. Repeat several times in a rhythmic fashion.

Several men who tried this said it helped revive a flagging erection faster than anything they'd ever done. One
said: "As a variation, I started with both rings in the center
of the shaft and moved them in opposite directions, one to
the head, one toward the base, then brought them back to
the middle and repeated."

• *THE BASE CARESS.*   Slowly caress the base of your
penis, squeezing the shaft and massaging the base.

• *THE SLOW SINGLE STROKE.*   Take the penis in one
hand and stroke slowly up and down the shaft. Vary the pressure.

- *THE FAST SINGLE STROKE.* Take the penis in one hand and stroke quickly up and down the shaft. Vary the pressure.

- *CIRCLE STROKE.* Circle the head of the penis with the flat of your hand.

- *THE SLOW TWO-HAND STROKE.* Use both hands on the shaft to perform the up-and-down stroke in slow motion. Again, vary the pressure.

- *THE FAST TWO-HAND STROKE.* Use both hands on the shaft to perform the up-and-down stroke quickly. Again, vary the pressure.

- *THE STROKE AND HOLD.* Stroke the penis up and down gently with one hand while holding the balls loosely in the other hand.

- *THE CUPPED HAND.* Put the flat of one hand over the head of the penis. Use the fingers of the other hand to stroke the shaft. Vary the pressure and speed.

- *THE CUP AND STRETCH.* While performing the cupped hand stroke, use the other hand to pull, or stretch, the balls away from the body.

- *THE FINGER STROKE.* Grasp the base of the penis with one hand. Run the fingers of the other hand up and down the shaft, varying the speed and pressure.

- *THE WRIST PUMP.* Put your hand around the top third of the penis, resting a finger or thumb on the ridge surrounding the head. Pump your wrist so that the hand vibrates the penis.

- *THE SLAP.* Gently "slap" the penis back and forth between both hands.

• *THE BEAT.*   Lay the penis against one hand and lightly slap the other hand against it, as if you were spanking it, or as a male friend says, "beating the meat."

• *THE RUB.*   Grasp the penis firmly at the base and rub the head against a pillow, the sofa, or whatever surface is available.

• *THE NO-HANDS RUB.*   Without using your hands, rub the penis, both shaft and head, against a pillow, sofa, bed, or whatever surface is available.

• *THE SQUEEZE STROKE.*   At the end of a single-hand up-and-down stroke, lightly squeeze the head of the penis.

• *THE SQUEEZE/MASSAGE.*   Slowly caress the base of your penis, squeezing the shaft. Then massage the base at the same time you squeeze the shaft. (This is a variation of the base caress, in which the penis is squeezed and *then* massaged.)

A male friend said, "This variation on the old Masters and Johnson squeeze technique is less painful and intrusive than the squeeze—and yet works as a delaying stroke."

• *THE OPEN-HAND STROKE.*   Lay your penis in the palm of your hand and close your fingertips lightly around it. Use a slow, light stroke while keeping the hand open, fingers loosely curling around the penis. This feels more like a caress than a stroke.

• *THE VAGINA SIMULATOR STROKE.*   Use anything that resembles a vagina in general feeling and hold it around your penis as you stroke. A banana peel is good. Some men surround the penis with tissue or paper towel dampened in warm water.

$\mathcal{M}$ASTURBATION AS A LEARNING TECHNIQUE

"I had to unlearn some of the masturbation techniques I'd always used," said Jake, a divorced man in his late thirties. "When I was a kid, I masturbated quickly to get it over with before someone heard me. And when I was married, I masturbated quickly to get it over with so my wife wouldn't wonder what I was doing in the bathroom. I felt guilty about masturbating all my life, especially during my marriage. I know she would have been hurt and offended if she'd known I was masturbating while she was lying in bed alone."

The dirty little secret in many marriages is masturbation. Couples believe they shouldn't need to masturbate after marriage or living together because they have each other. Shouldn't one partner be everything the other needs?

No one can fulfill every sexual need of the other person. Masturbation is a normal, healthy sex practice for married couples as well as singles. Most people do continue to masturbate at least occasionally after marriage for a variety of reasons, including the desire sometimes for a quick release.

"My wife always took a long time to reach orgasm," Jake said. "Sometimes I wanted a quick release, not a long lovemaking session."

Other men may want more sex than their partners do. (This works both ways, of course. Sometimes women want more sex than their partners do.) They simply may not be in the mood to reach out to their partners for love and comfort, wanting only orgasm without the emotional trappings.

Yet, like Jake, many men who masturbate when they have regular partners do so in the same furtive, guilty, and hurried manner they used as adolescents.

"After my divorce, I wasn't ready to date for a while," he said. "Masturbation was my only sexual outlet. One night I asked myself why I was rushing through the experience. Suddenly I had all the time in the world."

Using the strokes on pages 74–76 in a variety of combinations, Jake learned more about his sexual responses than he'd ever known.

"I am in a new relationship now," he said. "I'm a better lover with this woman than I have ever been. And I attribute that to what I've learned while masturbating. After I deliberately slowed down, I practiced combinations of strokes that enabled me to sustain an erection for longer periods of time."

Other men have had similar experiences. But you don't have to be between partners to practice masturbation as a learning path to becoming a better lover. Nor do you have to be a man. Women can use these strokes on their partners, too.

"My wife learned how to perform these techniques on me," said Carl. "She is adept at them now. It's very exciting for me to be manually stimulated by her. Sometimes we masturbate each other. This hand play has opened up our sex life and at the same time taken the performance onus off me."

Part 3

LOVEPLAY

Chapter Six

KISSING

I didn't think I wanted to have sex with him until he kissed me," Jenny said about her lover. "He didn't begin kissing in the obvious way, using The Kiss as the big wet prelude to The Fore-play.

"One hand caressed my cheek, the other held the back of my neck. He kissed me, playfully at first. Lips only, mouths loose, we brushed lips, licked lips. We were finding each other. Only when it was obvious something was stirring in me did he kiss harder. Passionately, we pushed against each other until closed teeth felt like a barrier that had to be passed. I wanted him in me. He rolled his tongue over my lips and pressed gently with the tip until they opened to him.

"My tongue met his and his withdrew into his mouth, playing hide-and-seek, making me find it. I raced in circles inside him, then pulled out my tongue, withdrew my mouth, and sucked his lower lip. His hand on my neck tightened and he took back my mouth, first with his lips, then his tongue. Slowly he thrust his tongue deeply in and out. I reached for his cock with my hand.

"All he had to do was kiss me and I was initiating the sex."

* * *

A kiss can be a token of affection exchanged between friends and relatives or an expression of passion in which the tongue and lips become sexual organs. Deep kissing is typically the first erotic act between lovers. The ancient erotic works including *The Kama Sutra* and *The Perfumed Garden* were eloquent and detailed on the subject of passionate kissing.

In *The Perfumed Garden,* Sheikh Nefzawi wrote: "Kisses, nibblings, sucking of lips . . . and the drinking of passion-loaded spittle are things which ensure a durable affection."

In our own time, the film many Americans of all ages regard as the most romantic ever made is *Casablanca.* We never saw the stars, Humphrey Bogart and Ingrid Bergman, make love, but oh, that kiss.

$\mathcal{T}$HE KISS

The *essential* kiss. If you don't like the way someone kisses or responds to your kisses, you're probably not going to find him or her an exceptional lover. Maybe not even an adequate lover. The women and men I've interviewed concur in the significance of the kiss. On no other subject have I found such uniform agreement. The kiss is the place where you discover whether or not the spark of attraction will catch fire. If that kiss doesn't burst into flames, why bother?

The kiss is critical, so intimate that often prostitutes won't let their clients kiss them on the lips. The mouth is an erotic organ, visible, accessible, yet *that* private. Many men also believe the kiss is one of the signs of compatibility or of love.

"I am not going to tell you I'm so sensitive that I won't make love to a woman whose kiss doesn't inspire me," said one man. "But I will avoid kissing her as much as possible and probably won't make love to her again."

Even scientists tell us that kissing is a form of personal chemistry, biological signals sent through the chemicals in our saliva. A good kiss is one of the Tantric signs of harmony. If you like your lover's taste and scent and feel you have come home in his or her arms and you find both healing and passion in the kiss, then you have found your mate.

There are physiological explanations for the power of the kiss. The sensitive nerve endings on the lips and tongue and elsewhere inside the mouth react quickly to erotic stimulation. The tactile sensation varies greatly with the amount of pressure and suction used. And the olfactory nerve cells in the nose are near the mouth. We really do taste, touch, and smell each other in a deep kiss.

According to Oriental erotology, the upper lip of the female is linked with her clitoris and the lower lip of the male is linked with his penis. This is a claim not supported by modern science. But it did give me an excuse to study The Kiss from two perspectives, his and hers.

Finding kissing experts was not easy. Sex gurus have theories and advice about kissing, but give little personal instruction. Call girls don't do it on the lips, so you can't ask them. Even books on the subject—often those tiny pretty books placed near registers to capture the impulse buyer—are devoted to such subjects as romantic spots for kissing or famous kisses in history and literature. I couldn't find a kissing seminar in any of my class bulletins. How can an erotic art be so essential yet so rarely taught?

I did find gigolos and some former sex surrogates, people who understand the arousal power of a kiss.

His Kiss

Michel is one of those men about whom Americans typically ask, "But what does he *do?*" Meaning, where does his money come from?

"Everything I have has come through the generosity of women," he said—and he has rather a lot: a large apartment in Paris, a small one in Manhattan, a farm in Scotland, a collection of modern art, and *clothes*. "Women," he added superfluously, "have been good to me."

In Europe, the life of a gigolo carries less stigma than it does in the United States. ("One assumes there will be elegant, beautiful men with no money who love women and one wants to be with them anyway," a French woman patiently explained. "Would one expect them to come to a party in something they bought off the rack and leave early because they must be at work the next day? No.") Rarely does a woman hand a man like Michel cold cash. Rather, she expresses her gratitude through buying him pieces of art or jewelry or perhaps a car or arranges for her investment banker to "set something up" in his name. When they travel together, she discreetly picks up the tabs with her array of platinum cards.

I met Michel through Vivian, an acquaintance who is part of the international jet set. Many of her friends had "spent time with him," she assured me, and if I wanted to talk to an expert in the kissing of women, Michel was my man. As she would say, she "put us together" over drinks at the Oak Bar. For several minutes they exchanged gossip about love affairs and the quality of their friends' most recent lifts—face, eyelids, neck, tummy, buttocks, thighs, and other places surgeons in Europe or Rio de Janeiro have no qualms about lifting—even fingers, and don't ask how they pull the skin taut on hands. Then, with twin sets of air kisses blown past both sides of our faces, she left us alone.

"The kiss," Michel said, lifting my hand to his lips, "is scared. A man enters a woman's soul through her lips."

Does he believe kissing matters more to women than it does to men?

"Yes, because men are not as sensual and sensitive as women are. Men are driven by power needs, especially American men. They don't take the time to enjoy being kissed. But women do. No matter how busy a woman, she has the time to be kissed properly."

A proper kiss from Michel takes some time. Before having intercourse with a woman for the first time, he spends two hours kissing her lips and body. Two hours.

Has anyone ever asked him to stop at ten or fifteen minutes on the lips and go on home?

"Never," he said, turning over my hand and applying his lips deliciously to my wrist.

"The French kiss is not a matter of pushing your whole tongue straight into her mouth," Michel warned. "One explores delicately, with the tip of the tongue first. Even if you are pressing hard with your lips, your tongue is not being forced upon her. A man can rape with his tongue. One must have balance and control. The lips press as the tongue darts and strokes and licks. If you produce too much saliva, you must learn to swallow some of it discreetly while you're kissing."

Reluctantly, I left his demonstration to Cara, a friend selected for this assignment because she "rarely" reaches orgasm via any means other than masturbating with a vibrator. A self-described "no-nonsense woman," she had more than enough doubts about the power of a gigolo's kiss to transport her to orgasmic heaven to make her an ideal candidate for evaluating the program. (I was already predisposed to be transported by his kissing of my wrist.) Imagine my surprise when she later reported that her two-hour kissing session with Michel was better than an afternoon with her vibrator *and* a day at the spa.

"If my boyfriend would spend only half this time kissing me even once or twice a month, I would be a deliriously happy woman," she said. "No wonder women shower Michel with gifts. Being kissed by him is such a languid erotic experience. After the first fifteen minutes, I was no longer aware of my surroundings. I could have sworn I felt tropical breezes and heard the ocean pounding in my ears. I felt adored and pampered as well as aroused and satisfied."

Can a woman kiss a man in the same way?

Yes and—Michel's assertions to the contrary—he will enjoy it as much as she does.

"When Cara told me she was going to try a gigolo's kiss on me, I thought, 'This woman has got to stop reading those magazines,'" Steven joked. "What a wonderful surprise. I've never been kissed like this before. It was the most sensual and erotic experience of my life. We have both agreed to spend more time kissing and not rush to intercourse as we had been doing."

Michel's Two-Hour Kiss

• Kiss the inside of her wrist first. You will feel her pulse, which will heat your lips.

• Brush your lips across hers lightly. Pull back. Take her face in your hands. Put your lips on hers and press gently as you look into her eyes.

• Devote several minutes to exploring her lips one at a time. Your kisses should be light, playful, teasing.

• Close your eyes and kiss her passionately—without inserting your tongue into her mouth.

• Discover her erogenous zones with your mouth, beginning with the back of her neck. They include armpits, inside the elbows, inner thighs, knees, the lower spine, breast, and genitals.

• Kiss and lick and suck her breasts until she is moaning with desire. Pay special attention to her nipples. Alternate the rough side of your tongue (the top) with the smooth (the underside) to create different sensations.

• Move back to her mouth. French-kiss her. Remember to use the tongue lightly. With the tip of your tongue, play with her tongue, the inside of her lips, the edges of her teeth. Don't thrust your tongue forcefully into her mouth.

• Perform cunnilingus until she has reached orgasm.

You don't need to kiss below the neck if time is short. Try the abbreviated form of Michel's kiss before leaving for work in the morning or before going out of town on business. Your reunion will be greatly anticipated by both parties.

*H*ER KISS

Can you really teach a man to kiss?

"Absolutely!" said Catherine in a clear, upbeat voice, which made me think of a popular morning talk-show hostess. "Oh, absolutely! I have taught many, many men to kiss. Some were flabby kissers, the worst kind, when they came to me. I turned them into delightful kissers."

A flabby kisser applies his lips to yours as if he were a piece of red meat and you were a black eye. He just slaps it on there and holds it in place with the assurance of one who is giving you exactly what you need. We've all known at least one. Worse, when they insert tongues, they do exactly what Michel warns against: They shove the whole thing inside. And if they drool . . .

"Too awful," Catherine said. "Most women won't kiss them again."

Catherine, a fifty-year-old California therapist who combines elements of Eastern mysticism and Western pragmatism in her work and her life philosophy, was a sex surrogate for eight years. She not only kissed the men that most women won't kiss again, she went to bed with them.

"My work as a surrogate was about healing through sex," she said. "My clients were men who had been traumatized by their sexual failures or had never learned how to be sensuous, to enjoy lovemaking. The kiss was the starting point. None of them could kiss worth a damn at the beginning, but they all could when they left me."

Working in conjunction with a therapist, she typically saw a client once a week—sometimes twice a week in the first month—

for a period of three to six months. Many of the men suffered from premature ejaculation, though a few were unable to ejaculate at all in the presence of a woman. (They could have an orgasm only while masturbating.) For various reasons, none of them had learned to be a sensuous lover until they came to Catherine.

"It goes without saying that none was in a relationship or they would have been working with their partners on their sexual problems together," she said. "They sought a surrogate's help because they wanted to learn how to be good lovers before they got involved with women again."

According to Catherine, a man's lovemaking ability in general is correlated to his kissing style. Improve the kissing and you improve everything else because you have taught a man how to slow down, taste pleasure, yours as well as his, and explore new ways of being sensual. That's why her first session with a new client was devoted solely to kissing.

"Kissing is an easy place to start, because his mouth is less threatening to him than his penis," she said.

Kissing has played an important role in the erotic lives of people throughout history in nearly every culture, Catherine explained. The Eskimo Indians and ancient Chinese actually kissed with their noses, not their lips. They applied their nostrils to a part of the beloved's body and sniffed.

"According to Tantra, there are nine types of kisses and nine places of kissing," she said, "and hundreds, thousands of ways of combining them into erotic patterns. If your man doesn't spend as much time kissing you as you would like, then it is up to you to make the kissing more interesting.

"Women are more likely to take the time to improve elements of lovemaking, such as kissing. Men would like to do that, but most don't know how to do it comfortably. Some lack the language for discussing intimate relationship issues. And they may be afraid of offending their partners by suggesting change in such an intimate area as kissing, which they regard as 'women's erotic work.'"

With their consent, Catherine gave me the names of two men with whom she'd worked as a surrogate.

"Catherine taught me how to make love," Rob said, "and she began the instruction with the kiss. I came from a religious background and married a woman just like my mother, which is to say, very devout and very afraid of sex. Then ten years ago at age thirty, I found myself divorced and with no skills as a lover. Our sex had been tense, hurried, and infrequent, maybe once or twice a month.

"I went to see a sex therapist after my first sexual encounter after the divorce. I had come in a matter of seconds. The woman couldn't rush me out her door fast enough, and I didn't blame her. I knew I had to get help or give up on having sex altogether.

"The therapist sent me to Catherine, who saved my life. That first session was an awakening for me. I thought kissing was pressing your mouth hard against another mouth and poking your tongue inside when you got the opportunity. Catherine educated me. But she did more than that. She turned me on to my own sensuous side."

The Ten Types of Kisses (The Tantra Nine, Plus the French One)

• *INITIAL KISS.* Like flirting with the lips. The tongue is used only to lick the lover's lips. This gentle kiss explores his feelings. It asks, Do you want to make love now?

• *THE TICKLING KISS.* Run the tip of your tongue around your lover's lips, inside and out, and then back again. Tickle, tickle.

• *THE RUBBING KISS.* Kiss softly, then rub your lips back and forth against his. You can use the rubbing kiss on all his erogenous zones.

• *PASSION FEATHER KISSES.* As lovers become more aroused, their kisses take on greater urgency. These repeated urgent but light kisses tend to be accompanied by increasing sounds, the moans, sighs, and gasps of increasing need and delight. The kisses are hot and fast, if the lover's mouth cannot rest long on any one place because the need to touch the next place is so great. A trail of passion feather kisses from his mouth to his genitals is a very effective arousal technique.

• *ECHO KISSES.* One lover repeats the other's kissing pattern, kiss for kiss. If he sucks your lower lips, then rubs both lips, you suck his lower lip, then rub both lips—and so forth.

• *SUCKING KISSES.* Most effective on individual lips, nipples, and genitals. The sucking should not be accompanied by loud, slurping noises. Nor should the pressure make the beloved feel as if he or she is being vacuumed. Light to moderate pressure is most erotic.

• *LICKING AND BITING KISSES.* Alternate the top and underside of the tongue when licking. Lick lavishly and bite gently. A love bite is a mere closing of the teeth or grazing of the teeth—not an actual bite.

• *THE FRENCH KISS.* Do not use too much tongue. If you push your tongue too far into your lover's mouth, you have less control of how you move that tongue around. The French Kiss is meant to be a passionate yet delicate maneuver, an erotic exploration of the lover's mouth and tongue with your tongue. Lead with the tip. Pull back. Circle your lover's tongue with the tip of yours. Pull back. Lick the sides, underside, and top of the tongue. Repeat, repeat, repeat. When you are both very aroused, thrust your tongue in and out in rhythmic, stabbing movements. Only when your partner is fully aroused should you search the recesses of his or her mouth with your tongue.

- *THE VIBRATING KISS.* In the midst of a passionate kiss, both partners open and close their lips quickly and repeatedly, like two small fish. (This takes practice, but is quite effective in increasing arousal.)

- *THE WATERWHEEL KISS.* Put your cheek to your lover's nose. Kiss his mouth. Insert the tip of your tongue and make a circular motion.

The Nine Places of Kissing

Ears, throat, cheeks, armpits, lips, thighs, stomach, breasts, genitals.

Eyes Open or Closed?

Studies show that 90 percent of women close their eyes while kissing. Only a third of men do. Why don't women look?

Men find the visual stimulation arousing. Women, the scientists tell us, use this time to fantasize.

"If women would open their eyes at least part of the time, they would connect more strongly to their partners," Catherine said. "Men bond with a great intensity by looking into your eyes during lovemaking."

Perhaps keeping your eyes open is a way of encouraging a man's kissing efforts, too.

George, another of Catherine's clients, said, "Before Catherine, I'd never been with a woman who kept her eyes open while she kissed. I could see in Catherine's eyes how my kisses affected her. That was very exciting for me as well as instructional."

Chapter Seven

TOUCHING AND EMBRACING, PINCHING, BITING, BUT NOT FOREPLAY

I asked him to put suntan lotion on my body," said Kelly. "He began by putting a few drops of lotion in his hand, rubbing his fingers together, and stroking my face. His fingers, soft with the lotion, glided over my skin from my forehead to my collarbone. Slowly he caressed me with his fingertips, then with the knuckle of one finger, and finally with the back of his hand in a circular motion.

"He told me to lie facedown on the towel while he put lotion on my back. Lying next to me, so close I could feel him breathing, though he was not touching me, he began to caress my back using one hand. He stroked me with his palm only, then the back of his hand, his fingertips, and the palm again. The pressure and speed of his caresses varied, moving down my back to my buttocks, making me shiver with anticipation for the lovemaking we would share later."

Kelly's first experience with her lover, Thomas, was a "sensual awakening" for her. At twenty-six, she had never been with a man skilled in the art of caressing, stroking, and fondling.

"He doesn't limit this kind of body contact to the warm-up period for intercourse," she said. "He is a toucher. I've been with men who were touchers before, but not like Thomas. He uses his fingertips, palms, and the backs of his hands in different ways. Sitting across the table from me in a restaurant, he can stroke the inside of my arm with one finger and make me crazy for him."

Apparently, Thomas knows how to perform and prolong the first act of love so well that it seems to stand alone. Our skin is the largest organ in the body. With millions of sense receptors—more than nine thousand per square inch—the skin is one continuous erogenous zone. In our haste to reach genital sex, we sometimes forget that the entire body has erotic potential.

THE PARTS OF LOVEMAKING

Shinzen, a Tantric master, told me that the act of love has three parts: a beginning, a middle, and an end. I met him last year in Bombay, through the famed Indian sexologist Dr. Prakash Kothari, who hosted the world's first International Conference on the Orgasm in New Delhi in 1991 and more recently the Third Asian Conference of Sexology. Dr. Kothari and Shinzen were discussing the linguistic roots of the word *foreplay* when I joined them at a bar in the plush Oberoi Hotel. A Western sexologist had incorrectly defined those roots in a paper presented at the conference that morning.

"Loosely translated, the term for the beginning is *for play*," Shinzen explained. "The middle is *swept away* and the end is *climax*. It is not necessary to experience all three parts every time."

"Ah," Dr. Kothari said, his eyes crinkling in amusement as he teased me, "don't try to tell that to an American."

Some Americans got the point.

The American modern model of intercourse contains three phases, as labeled by Masters and Johnson—excitation, plateau, and resolution (orgasm)—which correspond approximately to the three parts in the Tantric act of love. Our lovemaking is more goal-driven than that prescribed by the Oriental erotic philosophies. The goal is intercourse ending in orgasm. We have perverted *for play* into *foreplay*, turning sensual pleasure into the warm-up phase, which until recently was largely considered something the more easily aroused male did for his female partner, to bring her up to speed. She touched him sparingly so as not to arouse him to the point of premature ejaculation.

Masters and Johnson, however, replaced the word *foreplay* with *excitation phase* and later *noncoital sex play,* in part to lessen the pressure on couples to move as quickly as possible in a straight line from start to goal. Sex, they said, can be enjoyable before, during, after, or *without* coitus—a revolutionary concept. For treating female sexual dysfunction, inorgasmia, they developed sensate focus, exercises in erotic touching and caressing, in which the couples stop short of intercourse. Sensate focus has been hailed in this country by therapists as an invaluable tool in helping women become orgasmic and couples become more creative and sensual in their lovemaking.

Sensate focus

In the initial stages of sex therapy, couples are instructed not to have intercourse. Instead they are given homework assignments, series of pleasurable sensuous interactions called "nondemand exercises." They are not demanding because they are not expected to lead to intercourse or orgasm.

Couples who feel some of the magic has gone out of their lovemaking might profit from practicing a little sensate focus.

"We decided to go back to square one," said Julie. "In the beginning of our relationship we spent a lot of time kissing and stroking and massaging each other because we didn't want to have intercourse right away. That was a heady, romantic time, which we've recaptured by devoting one night a week to sensuous loveplay that doesn't lead to intercourse."

The Basic Technique

One partner lies on his or her belly. The other uses hands and lips to kiss, caress, and stroke the skin. Each concentrates on the feelings of touch and nothing else. How does it feel to him when he rubs her back with the flat of his hand? How does it feel to her? The partner being touched can ask for a change in pressure or speed of touch. And she is encouraged to let her partner know what feels particularly good.

When she is ready, she rolls over. Her partner kisses, caresses, and strokes the front of her body—except her genitals.

They change places and repeat the exercises.

Later, they add genital caressing.

"Few people realize that sensate focus is derived from the more varied and often more subtle arousal techniques taught by Oriental sexologists hundreds of years ago," Dr. Kothari reminded me.

And he is right. Everything we have "discovered" about sexual pleasure in the latter half of this century has actually been a rediscovery of ancient erotic traditions, adapted for modern thinking and living.

"I teach the time-honored techniques," said Shinzen, "which are kept alive now by Western interest in them, not by Eastern practice of them. The modern sexual repression in the lands of the *Kama Sutra* and the writings of Chopel and *The Perfumed Garden* have kept entire populaces in ignorance of their erotic heritage." He shook his head and said sadly, "China is a great land filled with prudes."

Like all the Asian gurus I've met, Shinzen is a former monk. This leads me to believe that monks in Asia must forgo some of the daily meditation and prayer sessions while they dedicate themselves to the preservation of their erotic heritage. (On this point, Shinzen is inscrutably mute.) Once they have learned the secrets, they go forth and teach, not the multitudes in their own countries, but the wealthy Americans and Europeans who can afford private lessons. In Shinzen's case, the clients are largely Japanese courtesans, the modern version of the geisha, and European call girls, the kind who are flown between countries on the Concorde.

He specializes in the first part of the act of love, the "for play."

Mea, a Japanese courtesan who studied with Shinzen, said, "Most of my clients prefer to be caressed, kissed, and stroked to orgasm. They do not want intercourse. But they do want a slow, sensual experience, the kind they don't have with the women in their life.

"The mistake people make in lovemaking is to rush toward intercourse, barely paying attention to touch as long as erections are achieved and maintained and female lubrication is occurring. They grasp at each other. They do not caress. When men come to me, they are telling me they do not want the rush. They want to relax and enjoy the sensations. Some men do not even want to have an orgasm, preferring to save that for their partners."

Several of her clients have had a standing weekly appointment for years. She also has regular clients from the United States and Europe.

"An American businessman told me that he would love to be touched this way by his wife and he would love to touch her in the same way. But he is afraid if he did that she would be suspicious. She would want to know, 'Where did you learn this?' "

Mea calls her specialty "Oriental erotic massage."

THE ART OF EROTIC MASSAGE

The erotic massage has been a specialty of the Japanese courtesan for centuries. My sessions with Shinzen included Mitzi, a beautiful Eurasian woman with stunning blue eyes, coal-black hair, a perfectly proportioned body, and longer legs than the average woman. She worked in a house of prostitution in Tokyo until a European client, impressed by her exceptional abilities, set her up in her own business in Paris. Mitzi and I were naked on padded massage tables so that I could feel what Shinzen was doing on my own body and then see how he did it by watching him massage her. Later we took turns massaging him.

Massage is actually a misnomer—as Americans define the word. Not the average sensual and/or vigorous rubdown, this is *sexual activity*—meant to arouse, not merely get the senses tingling in a nice way. The touch is softer, the pace more languid than in the American form of massage. Shinzen's erotic massage would be regarded as manual foreplay by most people.

Using only enough ylang-ylang oil (from an Asian flower, but any lightly scented oil will do) to make his hands glide smoothly, he began by moving from the base of my neck, slowly down my back, over my buttocks, thighs, and legs. He caressed my ankles before gliding back up my body, this time running his hands inside my legs and stopping to gently rub my tailbone. The big gliding strokes continued. His hands seem to float over me, bringing heat to the surface of my skin.

Deftly, he broke the motion at the base of my spine and began kneading my buttocks. That stopped almost immediately, to be replaced by the padding of fingertips, like a spider dancing on my ass. I shuddered. The fingertips scurried up my back to my neck, where the thumbs made firm circles into my hairline.

Back to my ass now. The spider gone, the hands kneading. Then, *smack!* to the side of one buttock and *smack!* to the other. The slaps, more sound than fury, made me push my groin against the table. Then of its own volition my ass rose to meet his hands. *Smack!* in the center of the butt. His fingers pinched and squeezed my warm cheeks. I was incredibly turned on.

He turned me over. His hands glided in big motions from my neck down over my breasts and tummy, thighs and legs. He caressed my instep, then took each individual toe between two fingers and squeezed it lightly. I was eager for his hands to work their way back up my body and I squirmed. He pinched my big toe. Back up my body, his hands came, stopping at the breasts.

Shinzen leaned over my left nipple and blew puffs of air across it. With two fingers he stimulated the tips of the nipples, then blew over the right nipple. With the center and the mound of his palms, he covered the nipples and areolae and rubbed in circles. He walked his fingers from my breasts down the center of my body, through my belly button and into the edge of my pubic hair. I gasped with pleasure.

Taunting and teasing me with his hands, Shinzen continued to walk and pad, glide and stroke, and occasionally pinch and slap. His genital caresses were deft and smooth. He pulled orgasms out with his fingertips, then massaged them into my vulva with the back of his hand.

In a state of total relaxation, I watched Shinzen perform his erotic massage on Mitzi. He started with her breasts, using the palm of his hand as he had on me. He gently rubbed the nipples between his fingers, then squeezed, pushing into the breast, and massaged and gently pulled the nipples out. In addition to the strokes he'd used to arouse me, he bit Mitzi, twice on each buttock and on her inner thigh and the sides of her breasts—leaving no marks. (Later, when I asked why my flesh had not felt his teeth, he said he would never bite an American. There was always the possibility we might sue.) Mitzi asked him not to caress her genitals, because she would, she said, give a better massage to him if she remained in a state of pleasant arousal rather than satiation.

We stopped for tea. Mitzi and I were given plush terry robes. Our tea included saki, Japanese wine, and little sandwiches and cakes, English style. His was just plain tea, which he drank black and strong without sugar. When we had finished our repast and taken sufficient time to digest our food—"Very important," he said—we gave Shinzen an erotic massage.

Mitzi, the expert, taught me. Most important, we used a firmer touch on him than he had on us.

"Women are more sensitive to touch than men are because women have more pleasure zones," Mitzi said. "And women receive more sexual touching than men do, so their skin is already receptive. Women believe they should not touch their partners too much.

They spare the touch to prevent their men from climaxing too quickly, which they do not have to do. They need only give him more variety.

"Men tell me their partners think foreplay is fondling their penis for a minute or two."

We began his massage by touching our breasts to his back. Then we used the same strokes he had used on us, only with greater pressure. At several points, Mitzi leaned over him, using her hair to tease and tickle. This was not possible for me with my short hair.

When he turned over, she wetted his nipples with her saliva and blew over them. With her nails, she ran faint lines down his belly, stopping at the edge of his pubic hair. She put her tongue into his navel and rotated it while I covered his stomach with short hot breaths.

She climbed on the table, straddled him, and pressed her nipples to his while I kissed the palm of his hand by merely pressing my lips to his skin and flicking the tip of my tongue in and out, making a staccato beat against him. We stroked the front of his body from forehead to toes. She sucked his toes, pulling each one out of her mouth in such a way that it made a funny sucking sound.

Mitzi massaged, caressed, and stroked his genitals using firm strokes. In her capable hands, he achieved an orgasm without ejaculation. I watched his penis go through a series of dry contractions that seemed to last a long time. He ejaculates, he told us later, no more than twice a month, though he has frequent and multiple orgasms.

The Kinds of Touch

- THE GLIDE. Run your hands smoothly in long strokes that blend seamlessly together over large areas of your lover's body. Don't stop to rub, knead, or fondle. If you use oil, do so sparingly—just enough to lubricate your hands and help them slide across your partner's skin.

• *THE SINGLE-FINGER STROKE.* Most effective on delicate areas such as eyelids and ears. Also thrilling on the throat. Simply run one finger very lightly along the skin.

• *TEMPLE PRESS.* Stroke the forehead with the fingers of both hands from the center to the temples. Press lightly at the temples. Imagine your fingers are smoothing away cares—or headaches.

• *THUMB PRESS.* Use the thumb pad to press with moderate firmness on accupoints (see pages 50–51)—but use this touch sparingly, as punctuation marks to long glides and other strokes.

• *KNEADING.* Not as vigorous as the "dough knead-ing" stroke used in a regular massage. Use sparingly. You aren't trying to loosen tight muscles, even if your lover has tight muscles. Most effective on buttocks where you grasp the flesh into your fingers, then push it out. Don't pummel.

• *SPIDER'S LEGS.* A highly arousing light touch. Use the pads of your fingers as if they were spider's legs wander-ing up and down your lover's body. The touch is light, teas-ing. Pretend you are a spider barely touching down as you move quickly along.

• *THE WALK OF LOVE.* Walk your fingers around your lover's body. This touch is most exciting when you use it to move from one erogenous zone to the other. Moving more slowly and applying more pressure than in spider's legs, fol-low the highly charged pathways. (See pages 50–51 for the pleasure points, or plot your own path by observing your partner's responses.)

• *LOVE BITES, PINCHES, AND SLAPS.* An occasional bite, pinch, slap, squeeze—always done lightly in the spirit of play—intensifies arousal for some people. Slaps are particularly effective on the buttocks because they bring the blood closer to the surface, making the flesh more sensitive to touch. Some men and women enjoy having their nipples teased by love bites or pinches. And some people *hate* it. Running a fingernail down the skin can also be very arousing—or quite annoying. Pay close attention to your partner's reactions.

• *THE NIPPLE STROKE.* Use the palm of your hand to brush lightly over nipples, his as well as hers. (Many men have sensitive nipples—and many others don't know they do, because this body part has been overlooked on them.) Gently rub the nipples between your fingers. Squeeze. Push them into the breasts, then gently pull them out, perhaps lightly twisting at the same time. Blowing over nipples wetted with saliva creates a pleasant tingling sensation.

• *THE BREAST STROKE.* Women can use their breasts on any part of the male anatomy. Press your breasts against him. Use the nipples to tease with light touches or presses. (Men can do this, too.) Hold your nipples against his. Or take your nipples in hand and rub the tips against the tips of his.

A friend who has tried the techniques on her boyfriend—and he on her—said: "We didn't get the difference between massage and *erotic* massage until we had these instructions. *Viva là différence!* In the past we'd massaged each other using too much oil and too heavy a hand. It was okay, but not arousing. This, on the other hand, is very arousing. We both prefer being blindfolded when we are massaged so we can concentrate totally on the sensations. It is even satisfying to be the one doing the massage. Using these strokes makes you more aware of the way your partner's skin feels beneath your hands."

Mea, the courtesan who studied with Shinzen, added a few directions, which include:

- *DON'T TALK*. "Discourage conversation, because it takes your attention away from the feelings generated by giving and receiving a massage."

- *TAKE YOUR TIME*. "Go slowly. Beginners in Shinzen's classes tend to rush at first. The strokes should always be slow, unhurried."

- *REPEAT A STROKE TEN TIMES BEFORE CHANGING TO ANOTHER*. "Repetition is soothing. If you move too quickly from one stroke to another, the person is trying to anticipate your next move. That is not relaxing."

- *DON'T BREAK CONTACT WITH THE SKIN*. "One stroke should flow easily into another. This takes a little practice but is important. When your partner is turning over, keep one hand resting on him. Even then, don't break the contact."

GENITAL MASSAGE

An erotic massage typically includes genital stimulation, which may lead to manual orgasm or oral lovemaking or intercourse. When and how the genitals are incorporated into the massage depends on how quickly you want to move your partner to that point. Generally, an erotic massage provides the perfect opportunity for extending sensual play and prolonging the state of arousal by avoiding or limiting genital contact for the first fifteen or twenty minutes.

Sometimes a couple will decide that the genitals are to be left out of a massage and then find they want that stimulation after all.

"I offered to give my girlfriend a massage the other night when she was too tired for sex," said a male friend. "I told her I had the directions for this new and more relaxing massage technique. She said, 'Great, but I'm still too tired for sex.'

"We had incredible sex that night. After I had massaged her for thirty minutes, she wasn't tired anymore. She asked me to touch her vulva. And soon she was asking me to make love to her."

Technique for Manual Stimulation of the Clitoris

• The majority of women prefer a soft touch. Generate movement from your wrist only, not your full arm, to lighten the touch.

• Use only the pad of your fingers, not the fingertip. Lightly stroke above, below, and at the sides of the clitoris.

• As she becomes aroused, use a soft, vibrating, side-to-side motion, which is achieved by placing finger pads on either side of the clitoris, touching gently, and vibrating the finger pads. When she becomes more aroused, you can create a somewhat stronger vibration by spacing the finger pads farther away from the clitoris, pressing more firmly, and vibrating more quickly.

• As a variation, place one thumb at the root of her clitoris, or use your free hand to stroke her labia or inner thighs or stimulate her anus or G spot. When stimulating the anus, use a well-oiled finger. Insert gently just inside the rim. You can locate her G spot by inserting your middle finger into the vagina, placing it against the anterior wall, and making the tickling or "come here" gesture. The rough patch you feel when you wiggle your finger back and forth is the G spot. Once you've found it, continue tickling.

I gave the directions for clitoral massage to four male friends. They all reported that their partners were enthusiastic, orgasmic—and "begging for more." One man said, "The wrist action makes all the difference in the world. Why didn't someone tell us this years ago?"

Technique for Manual Stimulation of the Male Genitals

• Lightly stroke the perineum, the space between the scrotum and the anus, with your fingertips or finger pads.

• Move your fingers to the back, bottom, and front of the scrotum in a quick almost tickling fashion. Then cover the same ground in soft caressing touches. Alternate tickles and caresses.

• Fondle his testicles with great tenderness.

• Grip his penis with palms and fingers firmly near the tip and move your grasp smoothly down the shaft toward the base. With a less delicate touch than you prefer on your own genitals, though by no means a rough handling, use the fingertips or pads of the other hand to stimulate the head. Firmness of touch is the critical factor in this technique.

• Run a fingertip or pad along the underside of the erect penis, outlining the head and the corona, the ridge surrounding the base of the head, the most sensitive areas of a man's penis.

• By now, there should be drops of lubrication forming on the head of the penis. Massage the secretion in a circular motion around the head. Add some of your own saliva if necessary.

• Lightly pump the shaft up and down while caressing the head. There should be a distinct difference in the amount of pressure exerted on the shaft and the head, which requires a lighter touch. Unless you want to bring him to ejaculation, pump briefly, then stop.

The four women who tried this technique on their men also reported enthusiastic responses. One said, "I always thought I knew how to give the classic hand job, but I had never applied enough pressure. He was so appreciative and showed his appreciation by making oral love to me until I was exhausted. I'm eager to learn more new techniques now."

*A*NAL MASSAGE

Some couples may want to add anal massage to their repertoire. Anal stimulation is a source of erotic pleasure for many people. If you or your partner don't want a finger inside your anus, you may well enjoy having the innermost parts of the buttocks massaged anyway.

The Technique

• Massage the buttocks using firm strokes. Then use light teasing—even gentle pinching—strokes down the crack between the buttocks.

• Separating the buttocks slightly, massage the innermost parts with somewhat less firm strokes than you used on the outer buttocks.

• With your partner's permission, apply the light teasing strokes you used in the crack down to the anus. With a well-oiled finger, circle the anal opening lightly.

• Using long strokes, begin massaging the buttocks again, starting at the base of the spine and continuing down to the perineum.

• Massage the perineum with your thumb or finger pad, exerting light pressure.

• If your partner is willing, insert your finger in the anus and gently circle inside the opening. Two fingers may also be used. Again, if your partner is willing, you may rub the finger in and out in a simulation of intercourse.

"I alternated the massage with kissing my husband's buttocks and running my hair across them," said Linda. "He loved it. While he preferred not to have my finger inside his anus, he was very aroused by the massage, including playing at the anal opening and massaging the perineum."

And from a man: "My girlfriend told me that no one had ever massaged her perineum before. This really excited her. We discovered that she could have an orgasm by having her perineum massaged. What a nice surprise for both of us!"

The Obligatory Word of Caution

If you play with the anus, however, you can't put that finger back on the genitals without washing first.

Mitzi, Mea, and other courtesans keep a supply of lubricated fingers cut from surgical gloves for this purpose. They slip a glove over one finger to perform the anal massage, then discreetly remove the glove and toss it into a waste container. In this country, you can purchase finger cots, miniature latex condoms for your fingers, at sex shops. Use a water-soluble lubricant, such as K-Y jelly.

As long as you practice this simple precaution, there is nothing to fear from anal massage.

Chapter Eight

SEXERCISES

I use my love muscles to grasp his penis tightly during intercourse," said Janie. "I can make him come by fluttering those muscles around his penis, almost like milking him. I can intensify my orgasms by clenching and releasing them repeatedly as soon as I feel the first contraction. And I can even hold him inside me after he has gone soft.

"Strengthening my love muscles has changed the way I make love."

Janie discovered her "love muscles," or PC muscles, after giving birth to a nine-pound baby boy.

"My vagina felt like a canyon. I peed my pants when I sneezed. My doctor told me to practice kegels, up to five hundred a day, to get my pelvic floor back in shape. I was determined to have the strongest pelvic floor on the block. The added bonus—and what a bonus!—is how much better our lovemaking is now that I am a love muscle virtuoso.

"My husband is thrilled with the new me. He's much more excited about this than he ever was about the hard-body look I got at the gym."

When women—and men!—"discover" their PC muscle group, they typically react as Janie has. They can't believe how much better lovemaking is, how much stronger their orgasms are. And, they ask, "Why didn't I start exercising these muscles years ago?"

Even sexually knowledgeable people who heard about kegels a long time ago often don't practice them. This is a mistake. Whether you are a man or a woman, the stronger your PC muscles, the greater control you have over your orgasms and the greater the flow of blood to the genitals.

Perhaps you're wondering what a chapter on sexercises is doing in the loveplay section of this book. Kissing and touching and caressing and embracing are obviously forms of loveplay. They arouse. Sexercises put your body in a state conductive to achieving and sustaining arousal. And you won't be able to use some of the techniques in *Sexational Secrets* to best advantage without strong PC muscles.

*W*HAT ARE SEXERCISES?

Not nearly as demanding as aerobics, sexercises are simple sets of exercises that help prolong the male excitation phase, speed up or deepen the female excitement phase, and lengthen and strengthen the orgasmic phase for both. The ancient Chinese believed these goals could be accomplished by rubbing the groin and scrotum, massaging the chest and breasts, and waking up one's internal organs by putting all the weight on one leg and shaking the body. Many cultures have practiced some form of erotic meditation and the use of aphrodisiacs, both taken internally and applied to various parts of the skin, as the means to the same end. The *Kama Sutra,* for example, advised covering the penis in a poultice made from seeds, roots, and plants that had been boiled in oil to a sticky thick consistency.

In the modern West, we favor exercises to strengthen our love muscles over the use of aphrodisiacs, which have fallen into disrepute. The most famous exercise is the kegel, which has variations for both men and women. In the 1950s, Arnold Kegel, a Los Angeles doctor, developed these exercises for the pubococcygeus muscle to help women firm up the vaginal muscles after childbirth. Few people realize he adapted them from exercises practiced in India for thousands of years.

Kegels have helped previously inorgasmic woman reach orgasm. The increased muscle strength, sensitivity, and control also make orgasm more intense for most women. The ability to grasp the penis during intercourse, to play with it by contracting and releasing, adds enormously to the pleasure of lovemaking for both partners. (And mild stress incontinence can be cured or dramatically improved through strengthening these muscles.)

In the male, a well-developed PC muscle can give him better control over ejaculation, making intercourse last longer. Ejaculation can be delayed by proper use of the PC muscles. At the brink of ejaculation, contracting the PCs may strengthen orgasm.

Isn't it worth the little bother to find and strengthen those magic muscles?

EXERCISES FOR MEN AND WOMEN

- *KEGELS.* Locate the pubococcygeus (PC) muscle, part of the pelvic floor in both sexes, by stopping and starting the flow of urine. Start with:

A short kegel squeeze. Contract the muscle twenty times at approximately one squeeze per second. Exhale gently as you tighten only the muscles around your genitals (which includes the anus), not the muscles in your buttocks. Don't bear down when you release. Simply let go. Do two sessions a day twice a day. Gradually build up to two sets of seventy-five per day. Then add:

A long kegel squeeze. Hold the muscle contraction for a count of three. Relax between contractions. Work up to holding for ten seconds, relaxing for ten seconds. Again start with two sets of twenty each and build up to seventy-five.

You will be doing three hundred sets a day of the combined short and long and be ready to add:

The push-out. After releasing the contraction, push down and out gently, as if you were having a bowel movement with your PC muscle. Repeat: *gently.* No bearing down. Now create *kegel sequences* that combine long and short repetitions with push-outs. After two months of daily sets of three hundred, you should have a well-developed PC muscle and can keep it that way by doing a hundred fifty sets several times a week.

Comment from a woman: "Kegels do everything they're hyped to do. A bonus for me is that I get turned on practicing them sometimes." And from a man: "Doing this was my wife's idea. I felt silly doing them at first and didn't see how they could really make such a big difference. I'm glad I stuck with it. This has made a difference for me in being able to exert more control over ejaculating and finding I enjoy it more."

• THE BASIC YOGA SEXERCISES. The anus and surrounding tissues are highly sensitive to erotic touch. These exercises contract the anus to build heightened sensitivity in the area. Whether or not you participate in anal sex, you will benefit from the increased feeling during lovemaking. You will feel your orgasms throughout that part of your body, too.

The Horse Gesture. You may sit in a cross-legged yoga position or not, your choice. Inhale deeply and hold the breath briefly. As you exhale slowly, contract the sphincter muscles, pulling the anus up and in. Repeat. Do a set of ten a day the first week; build to twenty or thirty.

The Root Lock. This is a more advanced version of the horse gesture. Again, sit in the yoga position, if you are comfortable doing so. Or lie on your back with knees bent. About halfway through a deep breath, contract your sphincter muscles. Expand the breath and the contraction from the anus through the pelvic floor to the genitals. Men will feel a pull in the testicles and women a quiver in the labia. Again, start with ten a day and build to twenty or thirty.

A woman said: "I excite myself doing these exercises. Either they have given me more erotic feeling in the anal area—or by doing them I have discovered the feelings that were there all along. Whatever, I feel like my orgasms cover more ground now. A good feeling." And from a man: "I feel a little kinky doing these, but undeniably they have increased my sensitivity in the whole area of the scrotum, perineum, and anus."

EXERCISE FOR WOMEN ONLY

• *THE FEMALE SUPERIOR TILT.* Have you ever admired the way actresses in films ride atop their partners in that rocking and rolling way? They move in a sexual version of the fluid, confident, yet controlled model's walk. It feels as good as it looks. A simple exercise repeated twenty times a day for two weeks can give you greater control over your pelvic movements during lovemaking, which will give you greater confidence about how you look on top.

1. Stand with your legs approximately a foot apart, knees bent, pelvis tilted forward, stomach held in tightly, buttocks tucked under. Hold for two counts.

2. Release stomach and buttocks, tilt pelvis backward.

"This is the easiest exercise I ever did, so there was no excuse not to do it," said my friend Sally, who typically avoids strenuous activity. "Surprise! I got something out of it. When I'm on top now, I can pull my stomach in so it looks better without losing control of the movements I need to make to keep myself excited."

EXERCISE FOR MEN ONLY

- *The Testicle Elevation.* The testicles naturally elevate during ejaculation. By gaining some control over the elevation
process, you can also gain some control over ejaculation.
That control increases the quality of your erections and, in
some men, the intensity of arousal.

  Locating the right set of pelvic muscles for this exercise
is the most difficult part. Initially, tighten all the lower ab-
dominal muscles to raise your testicles. Practice raising and
lowering your testicles until you can easily do so.

  Later, practice using different muscle groups until you
have isolated just those pelvic muscles needed for the exercise. Repeatedly contract and relax those muscles until you
can see elevation occurring. Perform the exercise while
seated on the edge of a chair or standing with feet approximately eighteen inches apart. Work up to one hundred repetitions, two or three times a week.

  "I found practicing in front of the mirror very helpful,"
one man said. "Seeing that I could control the elevation of
my testicles to some extent made me feel powerful. I had
gained some mastery over my body. That feeling naturally
gave me the confidence that I could have more control over
the ejaculatory process, too. The value of these exercises is
as much mental as physical. Once you see what you can accomplish with your body, you naturally say, 'Well, I can do
other things I thought I couldn't do now, too.' As men, we
really fall into the trap of believing that ejaculation is inevitable and there isn't much we can do to delay it. Not
true."

Part 4

THE ORALS

Chapter Nine

CUNNILINGUS

I love the taste of female juices, the feel of a woman's intimate tissues under my tongue. Each woman is different in the way she tastes and smells and feels. I find the real woman when I put my head between her legs. And to tell you the truth, I think I find something new in myself each time with each woman.

"I spent an hour on the beach with Marilyn this evening, arousing her with kisses and caresses so that when we returned to her room she was ready—no, *eager*—to make love. I told her to sit on the edge of the bed. I pulled off her bikini bottom and spread her legs. Kneeling between her legs, I pressed my face against her vagina, breathed deeply of her scent, and kissed her reverently.

"She leaned her head back and sighed as I began kissing her, first on her inner thighs. Only an oaf goes straight for the clitoris."

Steven is no oaf. He is an American gigolo, the real thing, not the fantasy Richard Gere played in the movie. Thirty-one, six feet tall, muscular and tanned, his blond hair naturally bleached by the Hawaiian sun, he makes his living servicing the sexual needs of women at three hundred dollars an hour. About a third of his clients are "regulars," career women or well-kept wives who call him frequently or, in the rare case, have a standing weekly appointment.

The majority are tourists like Marilyn, a travel agent on vacation who told Steven, "I want to do everything on this trip—drink, eat, shop, and have fabulous sex—and I'm not leaving anything to chance."

"It is a myth that women who hire gigolos are old and unattractive or shy and desperately lonely," Steven said. "Some of them are very attractive, but too involved in their careers to look for, or even want, relationships. When they want sex, they pick up the phone. Some want more sex than they can get in their marriage, but they don't want a messy affair. Most are attractive women. Even the less attractive are very well put together. They take good care of themselves."

But are they lonely?

"No. Horny. If they want companionship, they call a friend or business associate and set up a lunch or drinks date."

Marilyn found Steven through the network of connections every travel agent has, which includes a sophisticated hotel concierge. I found Steven—who tips concierges, maître d's, limo drivers, and others who send business his way—by answering his ad in a city magazine. You can easily spot a gigolo's ad in a city magazine or alternative newspaper. He will describe himself as "masculine" or "virile," claim he loves to please women, perhaps mention his "discretion," and—the red flag—list no physical requirements of the woman who responds aside from "generous" or "financially secure." While other men detail their specific requirements—which are typically young, thin, buxom, and blond—the gigolo says "age doesn't matter" or, more blatantly, "from twenty to sixty" and "marital status unimportant."

How many gorgeous men aren't looking for equally gorgeous women—unless they are more interested in bank balances than body measurements?

Steven describes himself as "a man who loves women and sex"—a description that applies to the majority of gigolos I've interviewed for this and other projects. Whether they do "love" women or they don't is beside the point. They make anywhere from two hundred an hour to several thousand for a weekend. You don't

earn that kind of money by specializing in two minutes of intercourse in the missionary position.

"Cunnilingus is my art form," Steven said. "I look good, not
great, I have an average-sized penis, but what I do better than
ninety-five percent of the men in the world is cunnilingus. I get
some women who want to be spanked or made to crawl across the
room on all fours or act out any number of wild scenes. A regular
client—a high-powered executive—always wants to act out a submissive scenario. But when the scene is over, they want what the
other women want: cunnilingus.

"If you can't do that well, get in another line of work."

THE FIRST RULE OF CUNNILINGUS

Cunnilingus—the oral pleasuring of a woman's clitoris and surrounding genital area through licking, sucking, and kissing—is an
ancient and widespread sexual practice. The word comes from the
Latin *cunnus,* meaning "vulva," and *lingere,* meaning "to lick." Volup-
tuous women being licked by men and other women are the pre-
dominant art on the Hindu temples at Rajarani and Konarak built in
the thirteenth-century India. The ancient Chinese called cunnilingus "drinking at the jade fountain," the juices of which were considered the elixir of immortality. A couple thousand years later,
Chinese gigolos, called "dish lickers," a seemingly perjorative term,
and the jade fountain was questioned as a source of immortality.

Making oral love to a woman has only in the latter half of this
century been regarded as a normal and pleasurable part of mainstream lovemaking in the United States. When Alfred Kinsey was
conducting his research in the 1940s and '50s, fellatio was desired by
men, though only received by half of the respondents surveyed, and
cunnilingus enjoyed even less popularity. Recent studies as diverse as
the reader surveys in women's and men's magazines and reports published in the scholarly *Journal of Sex Research* show that up to 90 percent of people participate in oral sex, which in some states is still

against the law. (Georgia, for example, permits the marriage of first cousins, but not oral or anal sex, even within marriage. Both are considered "sodomy" under state law.)

A woman who has achieved international stature as an authority on sex recently told me, "I came of age in the fifties and had never heard of cunnilingus when I went away to college. In my freshman year I dated a graduate student who had spent the previous summer working in a coffee shop in Greenwich Village and was more sophisticated and worldly than anyone I'd ever known. We were necking, petting, and humping in the backseat of his car when suddenly he pushed my panties to the side with his nose and began licking me!

"I panicked, but fortunately I couldn't move. I was frozen in horror. 'He's licking my privates!' I kept thinking. 'What's wrong with him?' After a while the panic melted into something more intense than anything I'd ever felt before. I had my first orgasm from cunnilingus—and I didn't even know the name for it or that it was something other people have been doing for centuries. I thought he invented it.

"We've come a long way since the fifties. I do not think you would find a young woman on any campus today who doesn't know what cunnilingus is."

In many beautiful Oriental erotic stories, cunnilingus is described in metaphorical terms. The man is the bee, and the woman's intimate parts the lotus flower. The bee's ministrations cause the flower to open and eventually to secrete sweet nectar. Never does the bee dive straight into the center of the flower.

The writers of these stories understood the key difference between men and women: the sexual starting place. They never began their tales of loving with cunnilingus. For men, arousal begins in the genitals and spreads outward throughout the body, while the reverse is true for a woman. According to Taoist sexology, the woman is first aroused by the tickling of her hands and feet. Hindus began by nibbling the tip of her nose. Western men start with the kiss.

Thus the first rule of cunnilingus is: *Do not perform it until she is already aroused.*

Gigolos, lesbians, and other experts on cunnilingus—including some heterosexual men who just like to do it even if the performance won't add to their financial bottom lines—all say that heading directly for the genitals with your mouth is akin to walking past the hostess of a dinner party straight into the kitchen and helping yourself to the food before it has been served.

The Basic Technique

• Stroke, massage, nibble, suck, kiss, lick, and otherwise tease her body, avoiding the genital area until she is fully aroused.

• Put your hands on her breasts. Massage her aureole with flat open palms, then play with the nipples as you lick and kiss slowly down a line from her navel to the edge of her pubic hair.

• If her nipples are not fully aroused, switch your mouth to them and use one hand to trace the line back and forth from navel to the edge of her pubic hair.

• With your hands, gently open her thighs.

• Lick the line of flesh between her pelvis and thighs. Kiss and lick up and down one inner thigh to the area behind her knees. While you are doing this, use your finger pads to spider walk up and down the opposite inner thigh. Moving your mouth to the opposite thigh, repeat.

• Return to the line of flesh between her pelvis and thighs and lick. While you are doing this, use your hand to caress the perineum, the area between anus and vagina.

• Use your fingers to part her outer lips to make her clitoris accessible. Lick and suck the area surrounding the clitoris.

• Cover her venus mons, the point where the clitoris begins, with your mouth. Suck—using *gentle* pressure. Some women enjoy having this area lightly nibbled—which is nothing more than letting your teeth touch the flesh, then pulling back, touching again and pulling back—no biting. Other women find even this pressure too much. Let her response guide you.

• If her clitoris is well back inside the clitoral hood, exert minimal pressure with your fingers along the side of the hood to lift and expose the clitoris. You may need to keep one hand in this position until she reaches orgasm.

• Indirectly stimulate her clitoris by putting your lips around the sides. Hold them in a pursed position as you suck. Alternate the sucking with licking of the sides of the clitoris and surrounding tissues. The clitoris is so exquisitely sensitive that few women enjoy direct stimulation. If she does, she will let you know that. Otherwise, keep your ministrations to the sides, above and below.

• When she is nearing orgasm, cover the clitoral area with your mouth. Suck around the sides of the clitoris. Stimulate her labia with your hand or stroke her inner thighs or tease her nipples—or alternate these stimuli. And do not move your mouth until she has reached orgasm—unless you plan to bring her to orgasm via another means.

Variations

• Insert one or more fingers into her vagina.

• Massage the perineum.

• Insert a finger into her anus. Some women are highly aroused by anal stimulation. Be careful, however, not to insert that finger into her vagina afterward.

• Assuming she thinks she has one and can help you locate it, massage her G spot. Locate it by inserting your index finger into her vagina, the back of the finger against the anterior wall. Move your finger in a tickling or "come here" gesture. The rough patch of skin is the G spot. Massage it in a smooth rhythmic motion. The jury is "hung" on the G spot, with many sexologists saying it doesn't exist and a few vociferously insisting it does. Some women also swear by the spot. If she thinks she has one, she has one—a small mass of tissue (the size and shape of a small bean and slightly rougher in texture than the surrounding tissue) located about two inches inside the vaginal opening on the front wall of the vagina, the side toward the belly button. (The G spot has been most colorfully described by sexpert Susie Bright as "that spongy mass of tissue just above your pubic bone.")

WHAT IF SHE DOESN'T ENJOY CUNNILINGUS?

Most women will probably enjoy cunnilingus if it is performed well. Some women have inhibitions about receiving oral sex, which stem from their negative ideas about female genitalia. Others may feel guilty about receiving so much pleasure or be too shy to ask for what they want and thus settle for whatever they can get. And some have only experienced cunnilingus with inept lovers, men who have turned them off to the act.

"If your woman is reluctant to let you perform oral sex on her, go slow," advised Steven. "Get her aroused almost to the point of orgasm before you go down on her. A woman is most beautiful to me when she has surrendered herself to her pleasure. If you want to help her do that through cunnilingus but she's a little shy about this, bring her to the verge of orgasm first. She'll come easily under your tongue and want to repeat the experience."

Angie, who didn't enjoy cunnilingus at all until she met David, her husband, a man skilled in the art, said, "My previous partners didn't know what they were doing and I didn't know how to tell them what they should be doing. We were ignorant. The first time he made oral love to me, David took it slow. He nuzzled and licked my labia and delicately parted the inner lips to expose my hooded clitoris. Taking his time, he licked the side of the hood. Then he asked me, 'Do you like it this way? Would you like me to use more pressure?'

"He paid close attention to my responses and periodically asked me what I wanted. No man had ever said, 'Tell me what you want.' The others had approached my clit like they knew exactly how to handle it, but they didn't."

Position can make a difference, too. In the classic position for cunnilingus, the women lies on her back, legs wide open, her lover's face between her legs. For some women, straddling their lover's face works better because they are freer to move their pelvises and control the rhythm of his tongue's movement.

"I've known a few shy, seemingly passive women who shocked me by the way they responded to having me eat them out while they're standing," Steven said. "Having a man kneel between their legs and suck and lick may make them feel sexually dominant in a way they've never felt before."

Whatever the position, Steven's favorite moves would surely thrill any woman.

The Gigolo's Five Favorite Mouth Moves

• *THE FLAME.* Pretend your tongue is a hot flame. Run that flame up and down her inner thighs, her labia, and finally her clitoris. "Keep the flame flickering hot and fast around her clitoris," said Steven. "Don't let it linger long on any spot. It drives women wild."

Comment from a woman whose husband perfected the flame: "Yes, it does."

• *SUCKING BREAST.* Kiss the nipples and areolae with light, flitting kisses. Follow by gentle nibbling. Run your tongue in circles around the areolae and nipples. Make the circles faster and faster. Suck the nipple into your mouth, knead it gently between your lips, suck again, pull the areola into your mouth. Suck in more of the breast, as much as you can, and hold it firmly between your tongue and the roof of your mouth as you suck. "Be sure your lips cover your teeth when you nibble and suck," Steven warns. "You don't want her worrying about whether or not you're going to draw blood."

Again, this is an original, incredibly exciting oral technique. A friend whose husband has been practicing these newly learned skills happily asked, "Why isn't there a Gigolo School of Lovemaking for men? Suddenly I'm multiorgasmic during lovemaking and I never have been that way except during masturbation."

• *THE FLICK.* Once your partner has become very aroused while you are performing cunnilingus, use the tip of your tongue to flick back and forth rapidly along the top of the clitoral shaft. Then flick up and down the shaft. When she is approaching orgasm, flick back and forth across the tip only of the clitoris. Steven said, "Remember to use only the tip of your tongue and the lightest pressure, as if you were strumming Tinkerbell's banjo. When you flick across the tip of the clitoris with the tip of your tongue, make the touch even lighter, so light you think it's too light. It won't be."

Exquisite sensations. A happy tester said enthusiastically, "These techniques should be required reading for all men over the age of eighteen. They made me feel wonderful. And they made my boyfriend feel like the greatest lover in the world. He couldn't be happier with himself."

• *THE VELVET NO.* Use this technique on women who have trouble reaching orgasm, even via cunnilingus, or multi-orgasmic women who want a stronger touch after the first orgasm. Hold your tongue stiff. Put the tip against the shaft of her clitoris and move your head rapidly back and forth as if you were saying, No, no, no. Steven said, "You have to do this movement very quickly and at the same time be sure your tongue is brushing her clitoris as you move. It's easy to lose the target if you aren't concentrating. And, as in all lovemaking, pay attention to her responses. If this is too much pressure for her, she will be pulling away from you rather than eagerly pushing her body against you."

A friend said, "Men have tried this on me and it hasn't worked. Now I know why. They weren't keeping the tongue on the clit. That really is key."

• *THE LIP PINCH.* Cover your teeth with your lips. Pretend your covered teeth are a set of pincers. Quickly open and shut them around her nipples or clitoris. The open-and-shut movement must be a series of rapid and gentle repetitions. Steven said: "Sometimes I use my fingers as the pincers on her nipples while I'm using my mouth on her clitoris."

This technique is very effective, especially when fingers and mouth are similarly and simultaneously employed.

What Not to Do When Performing Cunnilingus

• Blow into her vagina.
• Chew, bite, or proceed in licking, sucking, kissing, or nibbling with anything greater than delicate pressure unless she signals through body language or words that she wants a firmer touch.
• Consider a few cursory licks "enough." It isn't.

*T*HE CHINESE LOVE SECRET

Chinese sexologists believed that men could obtain sexual nutrients from the three peaks of a woman's body: the red lotus peak, her tongue; the twin lotus peaks, her breasts; and the purple agaric peak, her clitoris. On each peak is a fountain, the heavenly fountain, the twin fountains, and the jade fountain, respectively. Lovemaking typically included a triple-play game.

"This game I reserve for my private life," said Shinzen, the Tantric master I met in Bombay. "I can tell you what to do, but I cannot show you the heavenly fountain, the twin fountains, or the jade fountain, because these should not be performed without love."

Game of the Three Fountains

- *HEAVENLY FOUNTAIN.* While kissing, caress your partner's tongue with the tip of your tongue. Sweep the tip of your tongue over the roof of your partner's mouth, over to the sides past the molars, and down the floor of the mouth along the inside of the teeth. Use the tip of your tongue to stimulate the root of your partner's tongue. This method of kissing produces copious amounts of saliva, which the ancient Chinese called "lover's juice."

- *TWIN FOUNTAIN.* Suck your partner's breast as if you were a nursing baby—lightly and rhythmically. Occasionally lick the nipple with your tongue. Obviously no liquid will be produced unless your partner is a nursing mother. The "drinking" is symbolic.

- *JADE FOUNTAIN.* The man kisses his partner's mon before parting her lips with his tongue. He sweeps his tongue along the walls of the vagina, then pulls it in and out rhythmically. When the woman is sufficiently lubricated, he moves his tongue to the clitoral area and uses the basic method of performing cunnilingus.

I asked four couples to play the Three Fountains. One found it "emotional, almost spiritual to kiss in this way." Two thought the heavenly fountain portion of the game "too wet." The women found the breast sucking pleasant to stimulating. All four said that sweeping the vagina with the tongue encouraged greater lubrication. One of the men said, "It's nice to know I can make my wife juicier this way. This is a little trick that will come in handy. . . . But the wet kisses didn't do much for us."

THE NEXT MIRACLE SPOT?

Many believers in the G spot recommend stimulating it with a finger or two during cunnilingus to intensify orgasm. I would be remiss if I did not tell you there might possibly be another spot susceptible to similar stimulation. The new miracle spot may be right at your, or his, fingertips.

The Third Asian Conference of Sexology held in New Delhi in late 1994 focused on the desperate need for sex education in India and other Asian countries and on hypnotherapy as a cure for sexual disorders, not the sort of topics that would lead to the next big hype in sex books. Buried in the program, however, was a paper presented by Chee Ann Chua, a Malaysian family-planning expert, who claims to have found a new spot, which when stimulated properly "replaces sexual dysfunctions with unfettered pleasure." He calls this new erogenous zone the Anterior Fornix Erotic (AFE) zone, located inside the vagina and on the wall opposite the G spot.

According to his paper, he spent four years researching 193 Malaysian women aged twenty-one through sixty-five for whom sexual intercourse had been "a nightmare of silent screams." Only eleven women in the study failed to lubricate and experience sexual pleasure within one minute of beginning to practice his stroke technique, he claims. He advises women to teach their husbands to incorporate the method into foreplay—or if this is a problem for their man's "sense of feeling about his prowess," they should do it secretly before lovemaking.

"These women were desperate, often suicidal, until they found their AFE spots," he told me. "Mere stroking of this spot makes lubrication easy and women achieve single or multiple orgasms during sex. Women must practice this technique since the vagina has memory-loss problems."

Memory-loss problems? By that he meant the same thing Dr. Ruth does when she says, "Use it or lose it." In women who are not stimulated to the point of lubrication, lubricating becomes ever more difficult to achieve. Just as a man can lose his ability to have an erection in midlife and later years if he has no sexual activity, a woman at almost any age can lose her ability to lubricate if she is never aroused.

"In lovemaking," Chee Ann Chua said, "the man should stimulate both the G spot and the AFE simultaneously, which requires only a clean index finger."

Wouldn't that be *two* clean index fingers? I asked.

Laughing, he said, "Let us just leave the clitoris for dessert and have the AFE zone as the main meal." He had, I think, misunderstood my observation that he was advising men to cover two spots with one finger and assumed I was trying to move the discussion back to the clitoris.

None of the women in the study was available for interview. Sexologists from twenty-six countries more or less ignored Chee Ann Chua, except for Beverly Whipple, the sex therapist and author who popularized the G spot as an erogenous zone.

"I am excited by this," she said. "Only I feel the technique could be perfected with more pressure of the finger than had been prescribed by Chee."

I asked some women to locate their AFE zone and stimulate them.

"Personally, I've had no more luck in locating my AFE zone than I did in finding my G spot," said Alice, who achieves orgasm in the majority of her sexual encounters with her lover. "The process of probing inside the vagina with my fingers makes me feel like I'm subjecting myself to a gynecological exam. My clitoris is right at hand. Why should I search for a magic button when I have one right here?"

"I think I found it," said Claire. "My lover stimulated my G spot and the AFE zone while he was performing cunnilingus on me and I had a tremendous orgasm."

Some women do swear by the tickling of the G spot, and for them the AFE zone may be yet another pleasure site. If, like Alice, you can't find those spots, don't be concerned. Everyone has her own paths to pleasure.

CAN YOU TEACH A MAN TO PERFORM CUNNILINGUS WELL?

Yes—if he wants to learn. Let's hope he does, because it is probably more important that he become orally proficient than it is that she become so. Because the majority of women do not reach orgasm through intercourse alone, cunnilingus is a nearly indispensable part of lovemaking, which requires skill. In the Western world at this point in history, the sexually sophisticated man considers cunnilingus a necessary part of lovemaking—and often the one sure path to female orgasm.

"I believe in ladies first during lovemaking," said Jim. "I almost always give my partner her first orgasm via cunnilingus. That way, I know she had at least one orgasm. I've been with women who told me long after the fact that they faked orgasms with me during intercourse. I have no way of knowing for sure if a woman is faking during intercourse or not, but I can feel her orgasm during cunnilingus. That's very exciting for me, and knowing she's come also lets me enjoy my orgasm without guilt."

What if your man is yet to be enlightened? I asked some women who claim to have taught their husbands or lovers the art of oral lovemaking how they did it. Here is their advice:

- *KEEP YOUR CRITICISM CONSTRUCTIVE AND YOUR COMMENTS POSITIVE.* And don't initiate a discussion about what's wrong with the sex while you're both naked in bed and having that sex. If there's a real problem, talk about it outside the bedroom. Otherwise, directions should be gentle and brief and given at the point of performance.

  Jane said, "I finally got up the courage to tell him, 'Honey, I love it when you lick my clit, but it's so sensitive when I'm aroused by you, could you be a little more gentle?' I said it just as he was moving down my body with his mouth. He heard me and he got it right. If I had screamed, 'Ouch! You're hurting me! Don't do it like that!'—he probably would never have done it at all again."

- *SHOW MORE, TELL LESS.* Also from Jane: "Wherever you can, show him rather than tell him. For example, take his head in your hands and hold it still while you gyrate against his tongue. Reinforce him with lots of moans and sighs and gasps when he gets it right." And Kelly said, "Masturbate for him so he can see where and how you like to be touched. And when he's performing cunnilingus, if he's in the wrong place, take his face in your hands and pull gently away from him. With your fingers, show him the place. He will have his face right in your pussy and won't be able to miss the message. Then guide his head back so that his tongue is where you want it to be."

- *BRING IN AN OUTSIDE SOURCE.* Read aloud outstanding descriptions of cunnilingus. Cathy said, "If you get into a habit of reading out loud from erotic materials, you can slip in the educational stuff without making him feel he's in school. I keep books and magazines by my side of the bed. We call it 'turn-on literature.' I don't think he realizes he got his training in cunnilingus this way." Or rent a video that showcases expertly performed cunnilingus. (Look for films produced by women, such as Candida Royalle's Femme Productions series.) Maggie said, "Get immersed in the oral part of the video. Pant and say, 'Oh, how do you suppose he did that?' Your partner will look closer and learn something. At least my partner did. Men do want to learn. They just don't want to feel like they're being taught because it hurts their pride."

A male friend told me he didn't know how to perform cunnilingus until his second marriage. His new wife educated him, in a gently way.

"When we were first lovers, I knew I wasn't getting the oral part right, but she didn't come out and say so. She said, 'We need to learn how to please each other.' She took a lot of time performing fellatio on me, stopping to ask how I liked different strokes and so forth.

"When it was my turn to go down on her, I did the same. I was the one who needed the lessons, not she. But she handled it so beautifully, I loved her all the more for it.

"Nothing gives me greater joy than burying my face in her and bringing her so much pleasure with my lips and tongue. She is such a juicy woman that her juices often run down my neck. I love it. I can't get enough of her, of pleasing her this way."

Chapter Ten

FELLATIO

*T*he first time I gave a man oral sex I' was only a teenager and he was barely out of his teens," Monique said. "We were eager and enthusiastic and unskilled. He preformed on me first and really turned me on, though he did not know what he was doing. His tongue was warm and wet, and by wiggling my hips furiously, I got my clitoris positioned against him enough to do some good. When it was my turn, I was a little nervous. What if he tasted bad, what if he choked me, what if I hurt him accidentally . . . all the things you worry about when you are new to this kind of loving. I was surprised and delighted at how much I liked the taste. It reminded me of caviar.

"And the power I felt over him when I had his penis in my mouth! I was a goddess. I could give him unimaginable pleasure, I was more in control than I had ever been in my life.

"Lucky for me, I next became involved with a very rich man who taught me how to perform properly. When he left me, I was the perfect combination of enthusiasm and skill."

Monique, Marie, Veronica, Babbette, and Simone, five beautiful French courtesans, were spending a weekend at a Manhattan hotel as the guests of an Arab sheikh, a businessman who was in town nego-

tiating a deal. Well-traveled women who have racked up more first-
class frequent-flier miles than the average American billionaire, they
are fluent in several languages each. These women exude class. They
can talk about the art and literature of more than one country and
are, with the exception of Marie, politically savvy. ("I hate politics.
In every country, the people are much better than their leaders. I am
a cynic about the political process worldwide.")

Centuries ago prostitution was a sacred calling in India and
China. Women from certain families were consecrated to service in
temples. Even courtesans and other "public women" were treated
with great respect. To encounter a sacred prostitute at the start of a
journey was considered lucky.

The French courtesans have more in common with the sacred
prostitute of centuries past than with the women who typically ply
their trade today. From Manhattan, they would be flown to the
sheikh's palatial estate, where they would "provide the erotic amusement" for a small party—a party that would last for two days. One
of the sheikh's daughters was getting married. The wedding and surrounding events would cost hundreds of thousands of dollars, including the $150,000 (at $30,000 each) the five French women
would receive. ("That does not include the costs of first-class travel
and, of course, the little gifts we will receive," Simone explained.
"The Arabs are generous with jewelry. We will leave with some nice
pieces of gold and silver, maybe some precious stones.")

"The men have to do something while the women are busy
with their own celebrations," Marie said, laughing.

Perhaps you are wondering, as I was, what these five women do
to earn $30,000 each.

"Some society wives are getting paid a lot more money for sex
than we are—and one doubts if they do it as well," Babbette said cat-
tily. "Surely you've heard about [Mrs. X], who got her rich man by
performing fellatio on him while he drove his convertible in South-
ampton? He was delighted for his neighbors to think him that virile."

"Everyone knows that Mrs. Simpson got the Prince of Wales to abdicate because she was an expert at Fang Chung [the oral sex technique she reputedly learned while living in China, see page 139]," Simone said.

"That—and the nanny-child game," Marie added. "Well, everyone knows she let him wear diapers sometimes. He was a devoted submissive and she was his loving dominant. What else would drive a man to abdicate the throne for a woman? Good sex he could have bought anywhere." She paused. "Have you heard how [another Mrs. X] got her man? He was married to someone else when she stole him away because she uncovered his submissive side. I have seen photos of him shackled to the wall in a white spandex bodysuit and mask."

Do these courtesans earn their money by playing dominant?

"Sometimes and sometimes we pretend to be submissives, though we only dress and play, we don't get hurt," Monique said. "But not such games with this group of Arabs."

"Fellatio," Veronica said. "Men want it. Most women don't do it well." She added, "Some Arabs are quite good lovers. They practice the techniques for prolonging intercourse. If you want them to come, you have to take them into your mouth and make them come."

"Rich American men are rarely good lovers," Babbette said, "because women don't insist that they be. They are in too big a hurry and no one makes them slow down."

"Fellatio," Veronica said again, instilling the word with magnificent power. "We are the experts. I got started in this business as one of Madame Claude's girls."

Madame Claude, now retired, is perhaps the most famous French madam of all time. Profiled several years ago in *Vanity Fair,* she is, like the Mayflower Madam, Sidney Biddle Barrows, a woman of taste and refinement who taught her girls to dress and act like ladies. She believed that men wanted and would pay dearly for a woman whose exquisite clothing and manners were matched by her sexual skills. And she was right. Madame Claude's client list was reputedly an international Who's Who of the rich and the royal.

"She sent us to fellatio school," Veronica said. "We learned from a few of her most trusted clients, erotic connoisseurs, and from a gay gigolo, who was a very good friend of hers. No other girls in the world could perform the art of oral love better than hers."

These lovely Frenchwomen were gracious enough to teach me and a female friend how to make love with our mouths—something we'd thought we already knew. But after three hours of working on dildoes of various sizes, our thirst slaked by—what else?—the finest French champagne, we learned several new—to us, that is—tricks of the tongue and lips. Our lovers could not have been more delighted with the results of our adult education.

"You should help Susan with her research more often," my friend's man told her. He sent both of us huge bouquets of flowers.

FELLATIO

The ancient Chinese called fellatio "kissing the jade stalk" or "playing the flute." Fellatio by any other name has been practiced by heterosexual couples and homosexual men throughout history. In the *Kama Sutra,* it is called *auparishtaka* or "mouth congress." After her mouth has quickened his shaft, the book tells us, he cries out in *sangara,* the male cry interpreted as feeling joyously "swallowed up." Scenes of fellatio decorate the tombs of Egyptian rulers. And Cleopatra's skill in fellatio was famed in the Roman world.

The word *fellatio* derives from the Latin *fellare,* meaning "to suck," and has long been the erotic art form of courtesans and queens. In our time, an anonymous woman brought it into every suburban woman's bedroom.

She couldn't write very well. Her advice on love—it's part of life for a man, all of life for a woman—was dated when she wrote it. But how many baby-boom women learned how to perform fellatio by practicing on a green banana, a copy of *The Sensuous Woman,* by the elusive "J" in hand? *The Sensuous Woman,* first published in 1969 and reissued many times in the ensuing years, boldly instructed nice girls in the fine art of oral pleasuring. Best of all, she made it sound like fun, not some odious chore or the price one pays for diamonds and furs or even a roof over her head.

Sex surveys in books and magazines inevitably report that men would like more fellatio than they receive. (My own survey of a thousand men for the book *What Men Really Want* showed that 75 percent wanted fellatio more often than they received it, whether they received it nearly every time they made love or almost never.) According to a representative of PONY (Prostitutes of New York), fellatio is the most popular service performed by prostitutes at every economic level and has become in the past decade often requested than intercourse. Some men who use prostitutes say they ask for fellatio because they consider this a safer practice in the age of rampant sexually transmitted diseases than intercourse.

A successful married executive in his late thirties whom I interviewed for an article on why men use prostitutes said: "I see only top-of-the-line girls from the escort services and only when I travel. There is certainly less risk of contracting a disease from them than a street hooker, but I still rarely ask for anything other than fellatio." When pressed, he added, "Disease fears aren't the only reason. They take a lot of time in performing fellatio and do it very well."

His comments are typical of those made by other men I interviewed for the story.

"To be really good at fellatio, you must approach the penis as an object of worship, a fetish if you will," says Clarice, an American call girl who once worked for Heidi Fleiss. "Worship a man's penis and he is yours. Why should women rebel at this? Worship can work both ways in a relationship."

In ancient India, Shiva, the god of Tantra, was frequently sculpted with a generous penis. Sometimes his generous penis was sculpted without the rest of him and worshiped as Shiva Lingam, *lingam* being Sanskrit for *penis.* The *yoni,* Sanskrit for *vagina,* was also worshiped. Yes, it can work both ways.

The five French courtesans who shared their knowledge with me practice fellatio techniques that combine the straightforward advice by "J" and the more elegant caresses of the Tantra with an added French twist.

The Basic Technique

• Kiss and lick his inner thighs while pulling on the scrotum. Put his balls carefully in your mouth. Pull down gently with your mouth. Men find this downward tugging very arousing.

• Either with the balls still in your mouth or not, depending on what is comfortable for you, lovingly stroke his penis from the head down to the base. (Most men find the downward stroke more arousing than stroking up the shaft.)

• Get into the basic P-M (penis/mouth) position, the man lying on his back, the woman kneeling at his side at a right angle to his body. Take his penis gently in the palm of your hand and run your tongue around the head to moisten it. You can use a small amount of flavored oil to augment saliva, if necessary. Also lightly oil your fingers.

• Circle the head with your tongue, then work your tongue down the shaft, licking lightly with the tip. Repeat the stroke while massaging his testicles, gently pulling them down.

• Follow the ridge of the corona with your tongue while massaging the shaft with both hands, the penis sandwiched between them. Keep the fingers together. Use the palm of one hand and the backs of the opposite fingers to create a rolling pressure.

• Wet your lips and stretch your mouth to cover your teeth, forming a ridge, on top and bottom. Grasping the penis firmly in one or both hands, repeatedly move your mouth down toward your hand at the base of the penis and back up to the head, varying the speed.

Variations

• THE DEEP SUCK. Gradually suck into your mouth the full length of his penis—the slower the better. Move your tongue around the shaft as you're sucking in. Once he is all the way in, pull in the sides of your cheeks to create suction. Relax the back of your throat. Give the penis several hard sucks. Open your mouth to release the suction. When you close it, pull in the sides of your cheeks again before sucking. (Some men say their erections grow stronger with this kind of sucking.) If you can, tease the corona with your tongue while you're sucking. With practice, you may be able to lick from the corona down the shaft. To stop the gag reflex, swallow frequently. Also, it may help to keep your tongue flat against his penis.

• THE DEEP THROAT. Or, the deepest suck, which may be deeper than you prefer to go. Linda Lovelace's trick in the X-rated film *Deep Throat* was positioning her head so that her mouth and throat formed one long continuous passage, easiest done by fellating him while flat on your back with your shoulders at the edge of the bed and head thrown back. Experiment to find the right angle for you. When he ejaculates in this position, the semen goes down your throat.

A gay male friend who has perfected the deep throat said: "There is one other position [in addition to lying down, with your head off the bed] that works. Straddle him and kneel over his penis, facing his feet. Your throat and mouth will be at the right angle to accommodate his entire penis." *But* the Frenchwomen were unanimous in declaring the deep throat a "showy, not necessary move." Monique said, "You can be a first class-fellator without deep throating. Psychologically it is nice for the male if you do this occasionally. But your technique is better if you concentrate on the first few inches of the penis, where a man has the greatest feeling."

• BUTTERFLY FLICK. Flick your tongue back and forth lightly and rapidly across the delicate corona. After several flicks, run your tongue from base to head, then flick it up and down the same path, before resuming your ministrations to the corona.

• THE SILKEN SWIRL. Continually circle the penis with your tongue while sliding it in and out of your mouth.
  Also, combine the silken swirl and the butterfly flick, moving smoothly from one to another and back again.

• "J'S" HOOVER MANEUVER. The mini version of the deep suck. Using your mouth like a vacuum cleaner, suck the penis *halfway* into your mouth. While maintaining the sucking action, slide the penis back out.

• THE JADE FLUTE. Hold his penis firmly at the base in one hand. Hold the head in your mouth. Purse your mouth into a tight "O" and suck the head while playing up and down the shaft with your finger pads.

• THE FRENCH TWIST. This requires physical dexterity and those PC muscles again. Perform fellatio using the basic technique. Stop. Lower your body onto his erect penis so that he does not penetrate the vagina. Only your outer lips should touch him. Flex your PC muscles so that the outer lips lightly "kiss" the head of his penis. If you can support your weight comfortably by leaning on your arms placed on either side of his body, "kiss" down the shaft with your labia. Return to performing fellatio.
  "I was very awkward at this," a tester says, "until I real-

ized that the secret is in the way you support your weight on your arms. It's like doing half push-ups. Initially I was trying to control the angle and depth of penetration from my thighs. It's almost impossible to do that and still flex your PC muscles and kiss the head of the penis with your labia."

• *FANG CHUNG.* Begin by playing the jade flute (see above). Widen the "O" of your mouth and move to his testicles. Suck gently one at a time, being careful not to use too much pressure. Then suck the perineum while playing the flute and fingering the anus.

• *69, OR IN FRENCH, SOIXANTE-NEUF.* In this position, with either partner on top or both side by side, he performs cunnilingus while she performs fellatio. Most women will probably not be as proficient at fellatio in the 69 position, because a skillful performance requires some concentration. And who can concentrate when tongue is skillfully applied to clitoris? Like many gymnastic intercourse positions, 69 will probably look better than it feels, at least for one party. The angles are typically wrong for the most arousing clitoral stimulation, but the intimacy achieved is nice. Try alternating actively stimulating each other. When he is active, she can hold his penis in her mouth or even outside her mouth where it will be stimulated by her hot breath. When she is actively stimulating him, he can rest his mouth on her vulva or also let his breaths rather than his tongue tickle her clitoris.

Comment from a woman: "I like 69 best when I am lying flat on my back and my husband is straddling me. I can angle his penis into my mouth better that way. And he doesn't push too far into my mouth because of the angle required for him to make contact with my genitals. The position gives me more control—which I don't get if we're side by side—without making me feel like I have to do all the work of being on top."

What Not to Do

- USE YOUR TEETH, UNLESS YOU ARE DELIBER-
ATELY AND GENTLY NIBBLING AT HIS REQUEST.
To avoid scraping his penis with your teeth, be sure they are
covered by your lips.

- THINK THAT A FEW CURSORY LICKS ARE
ENOUGH. They aren't. There's so much room for creativity
in oral loveplay that you need not get tired of performing
the same mouth moves over and over. You can get almost as
much satisfaction as you give in performing fellatio. And he
will be grateful.

- CONCENTRATE TOO MUCH ATTENTION ON THE
LOWER TWO-THIRDS.   The head and coronal ridge are
the most sensitive parts of the penis. On the shaft, the raphe,
that seam running down the underside of the penis, is the
only very sensitive part.

- BELIEVE THAT FELLATIO IS REALLY THE MOST
IMPORTANT THING YOU CAN DO FOR A MAN.   I disagree with the French courtesans on the monumental significance of the act. Sexual skill is certainly important. But I
don't believe that perfecting this or any other one skill will
get a man to love or marry you.

*T*HE PERINEUM MASSAGE

Every expensive call girl knows how to induce male orgasm
by massaging the perineum. In fact, a working girl, a member of
COYOTE (Cast Off Your Old Tired Ethics), a prostitutes' rights
group, taught me this one several years ago and I was mildly af-
fronted that the Frenchwomen were surprised I knew it!

"Why would an ordinary woman need that?" one asked.

There are, for obvious reasons, more techniques for delaying male orgasm than inducing it (see page 183). Some men can prolong the ejaculation process by pulling and releasing the testicles repeatedly from the moment they feel they are going to ejaculate. I once had a lover who could make his orgasm last as long as a set of my multiples by manipulating his testicles—though he complained of tenderness afterward.

But sometimes a man or his partner wants to hurry rather than delay the process. He may have already experienced one orgasm during lovemaking, and relieving the sexual tension a second time may feel necessary but be difficult to achieve. Some older men, or men who are adept at holding back, may have prolonged intercourse to the point where ejaculation is difficult. Or, a woman may simply want some control over her partner's ejaculation while performing fellatio. This is one way she can be sure he won't come in her mouth— or that he will come when she is ready to received his semen.

The Technique

- With the flat of your hand or your thumb, massage the perineum—the area between the base of the penis and the anus—while continuing intercourse, manual manipulation, or fellatio. The key lies solely in the force of the pressure. Exert firm, not harsh, pressure as you massage. You are unlikely to induce ejaculation, however, if he is not very aroused.

  One woman commented, "The first time I tried the perineum massage, I was too timid. Later, he asked what I'd been trying to do 'down there.' Next time, he didn't have to ask."

Monique insisted the secret lies in finding the exact "prostate point," in the middle of the perineum.

"If you aren't sure of its location, press a few spots and watch his reaction," she said. "You'll know when you hit it because he will moan or move erotically. His penis will vibrate like a tuning fork. This is the male equivalent of the G spot.

"You can bring him to a wondrous conclusion by hooking the thumb and index finger of one hand around the base of the penis and pressing the prostrate point with the free thumb of the other hand while performing fellatio.

"Some men like you to touch their spot from inside the anus. You need insert no more than a fingertip to find it. Once your finger is inside the anus, move it around experimentally until you get his response. I have a way of doing this that is clean and does not offend my clients. I cut individual fingers out of thin surgical gloves so that I can slip one finger of a glove over my finger before I dip into the lubricant without the man seeing and knowing what I am doing. When I am finished I can roll up the finger and discard it into a discreet little trash bag, tucked in between the mattress and springs of the bed."

You can also stimulate the prostrate point during orgasm to extend the period of contractions (see page 225).

ℋEAT AND ICE

The late renowned erotic writer Marco Vassi told me that "Running Hot and Cold" was a "mild form of kinky sex." We were guests at the time on a talk radio program. This was the only time in Marco's bag of kinky tricks that he could discuss on air. (Some of Marco's novels, which are filled with detailed sex scenes, are still in print in trade paper and can be ordered through Good Vibrations if you can't find them in your local bookstores.) Following the show, I went straight home and tried a little heat and ice on my lover.

The Technique

• While performing oral sex, vary the temperature of your mouth. Start with normal body temperature. Then, using your hand to stimulate your partner, fill your mouth with ice cubes. Wait until your tongue is numb before spitting out the ice. Apply your frozen assets to your partner's genitals. This feels like a jolt of sexual electricity. After a few minutes, when your oral temperature is back to normal, repeat the procedure, this time filling your mouth with hot tea. This method of alternating temperatures prolongs the excitation phase for some men and causes others to have more intense orgasms.

Two women who tried heat and ice on their men reported the game was well received. "My husband said the rush he got with the temperature change was unlike anything he'd ever felt," Maggie said. "And I could feel that his orgasm was stronger when he ejaculated during intercourse."

There are other games to be played with ice alone. Some men report their orgasms are intensified if their partners slap a handful of crushed ice in the small of the back prior to ejaculation. Both sexes can be aroused by the pleasurable, slightly painful sensations created by a dripping ice cube held momentarily against a nipple or moved slowly up and down the body from nipples to genitals. (Never use dry ice or a dry supercooled ice cube.)

"I had a lover who used an ice cube to trace intricate patterns on my body after I'd had one or two orgasms and was hot enough to melt it fast," said Carol. "Sometimes he rested the last sliver of ice inside my navel while he performed cunnilingus. Delicious."

$\mathscr{S}$WALLOWING

If a man ejaculates during fellatio, unless he is wearing a condom, you have two choices: swallow the semen or let it dribble out the corners of your mouth, which can be done with a minimum of display. The amount of ejaculate is typically less than a teaspoon. Admittedly, it can seem like more if you aren't prepared for the experience.

There are genuine health concerns for a woman who does choose to swallow her partner's semen. Swallowing is not routinely practiced by prostitutes, call girls, or courtesans—particularly now in the age of AIDS and other sexually transmitted diseases—though some will do it, if only for a select clientele. If you and your partner are involved in a committed, monogamous relationship and neither of you have been exposed to HIV (the virus that causes AIDS) prior to the relationship, safe sex is not an issue. The only issue is whether or not you want to swallow his semen.

However, I would be remiss if I did not note in passing that many women believe they are involved in monogamous relationships when their partners are secretly seeing other women, including prostitutes. And some people do carry HIV or have STDs without knowing they do. How far to trust is an individual decision not to be made lightly. (You should not be performing fellatio without a condom or having unprotected intercourse in a casual relationship.)

How important is swallowing to a man? Like anal sex, it may be something he asks for because he's rarely, if ever, experienced it.

"My wife is the only woman who has ever swallowed me," said Dan. "I felt very loved by her the first time she did. It was her idea. Swallowing doesn't have to be a regular occurrence, just once in a while, as a special treat."

"It's not that important," said Anthony. "Nice, but not necessary. I don't think whether a woman does or does not swallow says as much about her feelings for me as it does about her skill and comfort level with fellatio. I'm not offended if she can't or won't swallow."

"This was something my lover really wanted," said Grace. "After we took the AIDS test together and swore to be faithful to each other and moved in together—well, I had run out of excuses for not doing this. I was afraid I would choke or gag. I called a good friend who is gay and asked his secret. He said, 'It's simple. Fellate him until he is close to ejaculation. Then deep throat him and massage his perineum so that he will ejaculate when you are in position. He will shoot straight down your throat, you won't taste, you won't gag.'

"My friend was right. I couldn't hold the deep-throat position for long, but once you know how to push the magic button, you don't have to hold it for long."

Yes, her friend was right. His technique is practiced by experts in oral lovemaking.

The Basic Swallow

- Fellate your partner using a variety of techniques until he is close to orgasm.

- Get into position for the deep suck or deep throat by either straddling him, facing his feet or lying on your back with your head off the bed. The mouth and throat should form one line.

- When you are ready for him to ejaculate, massage his perineum. The semen will slide down your throat.

CAN A MAN TEACH A WOMAN TO PERFORM FELLATIO?

Yes—in the same way a woman can teach a man to perform cunnilingus (see page 128). Men don't realize that women often suffer from performance anxiety, too, particularly in regard to performing fellatio. Many women have told me they don't do it because they're afraid of doing it "wrong." You need to let her know what you want without destroying her confidence.

"When I started seeing the woman who is now my wife," Jeff said, "she wasn't very good at performing fellatio. She licked me like I was an ice cream cone, long licks up from the base to the tip, followed by a few sucks on the head. I told her that she had probably been with men who were premature ejaculators and had learned to give them minimal oral attention, but that I could handle a lot more.

"She bought a book, because that's how she learns new things; and she was a quick study. I'm glad I was straight with her about this because it allowed her to open up to me about what she wanted in bed, too. I know I'm a better lover for her than I would have been without that kind of support from her."

Part 5

POSITIONS

Chapter Eleven

POSITIONING IS EVERYTHING

I like to watch myself in the act," said John. "And I prefer rear-entry position because I can see myself thrusting in and out. In that position I can pull back farther, and watching my cock pull out and push back into my wife blows me away. I didn't understand why she was so opposed to rear entry because I play with her clit and give her a big orgasm that way. One night after we'd been drinking a lot of wine, she told me that she didn't like rear entry because her breasts hang down.

"'They sag,' she said. 'They get all out of shape because they're so big. They hang down like elongated water jugs.' She was afraid I would look at them and be turned off. I hope I was able to convince her that I'm too busy looking at my cock and her ass when we're fucking from the rear to notice her breasts hanging down. And what's wrong with them hanging down anyway? If they didn't hang down a little when she is in that position, they wouldn't be real breasts. She has the most beautiful breasts I've ever seen."

From my years of conducting interviews as a sex journalist, I've concluded that the rear-entry position is the least favored basic position of women and second most favored basic position of men. Like John's wife, many women think their breasts—and/or tummies—sag in the rear-entry position. And many of these women are young and don't look saggy to me.

"I don't want it to all hang out when anyone is in a position to see it hanging, especially my lover," said a twenty-eight-year-old woman.

In spite of some female concerns about their bodies being too much on display, women as well as men rate the female-superior position their favorite.

"I like being on top because I know I can bring myself to orgasm in that position," one woman said.

"Great visuals and best room for maneuvering the female genitalia," one man said.

"I love the control," a woman enthused. "Besides, my husband is much bigger than I am. If I'm not on top, we have to think too much about positioning so he doesn't squish me."

The unfairly maligned missionary position is, I've found among those I've interviewed, surprisingly more favored by women than men.

How MANY POSITIONS ARE POSSIBLE?

"There are really only six basic positions for intercourse," said Dr. Prokash Kothari, the Indian sexologist, when I visited him in Bombay. He enumerated them on his fingers. "Woman on top, man on top, rear entry, side by side, sitting, and standing. Six only. Everything else is a variation of one of these basics. You would not think it would be too much to learn, would you?

"But in India today it would be rare to find the man who is skilled in six positions. India is a very sexually repressed country, more so than the United States. This may be the land of the *Kama Sutra* and the birthplace of sacred sexuality, but modern Indian men are not taught about sex. Very little material, either educational or erotic, is available to them."

Stonemasons, woodcarvers, artists, and engravers left testaments to the variety of sexual postures once celebrated in India. *Celebrated,* not necessarily practiced. There are over a hundred positions for intercourse in the *Kama Sutra,* most of them coming under the heading of "Why would you want to try this at home?" If you do try some of the more distorted poses, you may find the concept is more interesting than the erotic sensations created. There is serious reason to doubt anyone but the most adept yogi ever perform them.

Sheikh Nefzawi, author of the great sixteenth-century Arab sex manual, *The Perfumed Garden,* had similar doubts. His comment on a particular Indian posture in which the male and female contorted like pretzels with connecting genitals: "I think it is only realizable in thought and design."

Perhaps the artists of that time period had a collective overactive imagination and were making art to excite themselves. The images they created were copied in the art of the bazaars of many countries and have excited millions of people over the centuries. The ancient Hindus elevated sex to the level of sacred art.

In *The Perfumed Garden,* Nefzawi, in spite of his criticisms of Hindu positions, suggests a posture called "the mutual view of the buttocks," in which the man lies on his back, while the woman turns her back to him and sits on his penis. If he clasps her body with his legs, she leans over until her hands touch the floor—affording both a view of the other's buttocks.

"Only a man would think that was a brilliant idea," a female friend said, laughing.

Even the photos of lovers in today's sex guides show us positions that, while modified from the ancient drawings, can be practical only by two people with good musculature and no protruding bellies. Research shows us that at least half the American population is overweight and the baby-boom generation, the vast consumer market for all things sexual, is aging. There are bad backs to consider. Knee injuries. Tennis elbows. Late pregnancies.

"Each one of the basic positions will work in one form or another for almost any couple," Dr. Kothari said. "Only the very obese, one hundred or more pounds overweight, the very pregnant, or the incapacitated would have problems."

Are six positions enough? I asked him. Don't we need more variety than that?

"The positions can be slightly adapted. And you can do many things in one position—intercourse, fellatio, cunnilingus, and so forth. Yes, the variety is there. Most important is the comfort. If you are struggling to stay in a position, how are you going to make love in it?"

Dr. Kothari's following criteria for deciding if a position should be part of your repertoire.

The Simple Feel-Good Test

• Can you comfortably get into the position and hold it easily enough so that you aren't distracted from enjoying lovemaking by trying to keep your body in place? Do your muscles tremble from the effort of sustaining the position?

• Is this position conducive to female orgasm? (The majority of women do not reach orgasm through intercourse alone. Does the position allow the woman or her partner room to stroke and caress her genitals?) And/or does it aid a man in controlling the timing of his ejaculation?

• After it satisfies the primary concerns, ask, Am I visually stimulating to my partner in this position? ("Men are erotic visualists," he said. Where have you heard that before? "You do want to arouse them visually, but you are more likely to do that by becoming visibly excited than by posing artfully. Keep this in mind.")

THE CALL GIRL'S PRIME POSITION: WOMAN ON TOP

"The best position for intercourse really varies with the partners," Shelley said. "Their physical size, the condition of her vagina, the man's penis size, his degree of hardness, and other factors determine what really works best for two people. That said, most of my customers still want me to be on top. About seventy percent of the time, we do it female-superior style."

Shelley, who has a master's degree in psychology, is working on her Ph.D. A former exotic dancer and stripper, she is one of the top call girls in Los Angeles and got her start with Heidi Fleiss, a woman who knew talent when she saw it. Why would a Ph.D. candidate want to be a call girl?

"I'm good at sex and lousy at waitressing," she said, laughing. "I like sex. I have orgasms with my clients, because I know how to make myself come. They love to watch me come, they know it's real. Because I bring myself, I let them off the hook—which is why they pay me so much money, to be with a woman they don't have to work to excite, a woman who will joyously come on top."

Dressed in black tights, expensive black cowboy boots, an oversized heavy black silk shirt that could have been borrowed from a boyfriend, her oversized black frame glasses sliding down the bridge of her nose, with a college text on economics visible in her leather tote bag—she looked younger than her twenty-eight years and very fit. She works out eight to ten hours a week at a health club.

"I probably turned my first trick before I consciously knew I was a prostitute," she said. "I met men through the club where I danced. They took me out, bought me presents, gave me money. I had sex with them. It just took me a while to formalize the relationships and declare myself a business. I got into prostitution as a freelancer."

In the interests of being fair to other women, she said that most women who work in the sex industry are specialists. They don't "freelance" in other areas. Call girls don't work for phone sex services. Exotic dancers don't turn tricks. Shelley moved from exotic dancing to prostitution by commissioning one of the club's bouncers to arrange dates for her with chosen men—which most of the girls, contrary to popular belief, don't do.

"I loved the power I had as a dancer," she says "Men were fantasizing about doing all kinds of things to my body. I felt the energy of their thoughts. I was turned on by knowing they couldn't have me. I believe women are natural exhibitionists and men are natural voyeurs."

Shelley has approximately thirty clients, about a third of whom have weekly appointments. Some call her when they're in Los Angeles on business—maybe only a few times a year. A typical client wants mutual masturbation, each of them masturbating naked side by side in front of a full-length mirror for which he pays $350 an hour. Men who pay $1,500 for the night want companionship, romance, someone to listen and sympathize, a woman who doesn't bring demands or needs or problems of her own to the dinner table—and sex in the female-superior position. Shelley calls them "dates."

"Partly, they like surrendering control to me. They see a woman on top as a woman in charge," she said. "They are paying me to take charge, to pleasure them. Maybe they have to do the work with their wives and they don't want to do it with someone they're paying a lot of money. When men talk to me about their wives, they say things like 'I wish she initiated sex more often' or 'She doesn't like to be on top' or 'She doesn't like sex very much,' which I suspect means 'She doesn't have an orgasm very often.' They never complain about their wives' bodies—just their inhibitions.

"They like to watch me having orgasms, which they can do better if I'm astride them. They want to see my face change when I come. They want to see me sweat and my chest turn pink with excitement."

If you are a woman who has shied away from the female-superior position because you're embarrassed about being on display or worried about your sagging breasts or little tummy—put aside those fears. The vast majority of men aren't being coldly analytical about their partners' body faults during intercourse. Men tend to focus on what is best about our bodies and forgive the rest, particularly in the heat of passion. They are much more forgiving of us than we are of ourselves.

Shelley's Advice for Being on Top

• DRESS FOR THE AUDIENCE. "If you're worried about your tummy or the spider veins in your upper thighs, cover them up with a loose teddy and leg makeup. Dressing for bed is a fun thing to do no matter how you feel about your body. Men love it when you come to bed in high heels, bustier, and stockings. You don't have to be nude every time you make love. Clothes can give a woman confidence, even in bed."

• MAKE EYE CONTACT WITH HIM. "Men tell me their wives close their eyes when they come. But men like to see into your eyes when you come. Woman on top is a great position for that eye contact. You don't feel so vulnerable as you do when he's on top."

• USE YOUR HANDS. "Men like to see women masturbate. Don't shyly sneak a finger down there. Openly play with your clit when you're on top."

• BE A LITTLE DOMINANT. "Lean over and tweak his nipples occasionally. Give him some orders he won't mind following, like, 'Play with my breasts.' Kiss him hard, then pull away with your lips still on his so he has to reach to stay connected to you. Take his wrists or hands and push them above his head. Sometimes he wants to feel like you are really in charge. It relieves him of the pressure of having to make the sex good for you. That little nipple tweak promises you can make it good for both of you."

The Basic Positions

• *THE FEMALE-SUPERIOR POSITION,* or woman on top, is considered by sex therapists the most favorable inter-course position for female orgasm. She has the freedom to touch her clitoris as well as control the depth and angle of penetration and the speed of thrusting. Her partner can also fondle her genitals or breasts. In the most common variation of the position, the woman squats or sits astride the man, who is lying on his back in a riding position, her legs bent at the knees on either side of his body. She may lean forward, putting her weight on her hands on either side of his shoulders, or she may lean on one hand, or maintain an upright position, keeping both hands free. As she controls the angle and depth of penetration and the speed of thrust, he manually stimulates her breasts and/or clitoris. The position also provides visual stimulation for her partner. He can see her breasts and watch her moving and stimulating herself.

Bonus: Women who are not comfortable masturbating for their lovers may find it easier to stroke themselves while on top. Female-superior can be a very uninhibited position.

And: A woman can get the additional clitoral stimulation she needs in more creative ways when she's on top. She can alternate deep thrusting with using the head of his penis to tease her clitoris. Some women find intense pleasure in moving from side to side in a circular pattern. In the final stages prior to orgasm, she may flatten herself out on top of him, clench her thighs together, and roll her clitoris into him.

Best position for: a man with a small to average penis, because penetration is deeper.

Not the best for: a man with a large penis and a woman

with a short vagina, or a woman in the last trimester of pregnancy.

• THE MISSIONARY POSITION, or man on top, the other face-to-face position, has been unfairly maligned in modern times. Legend has it that Pacific Islanders named the position after the missionaries who used it. This is still a great position for hard thrusting and emotional contact. Many women as well as men enjoy making love this way— as long as it isn't the only way!—and find it more intimate than any other. In the basic version of the position, the woman lies on her back with her legs slightly parted and the man lies on top of her, supporting himself at least partially with his hands.

To lessen or increase depth of penetration:

A pillow under the small of her back can change the angle and depth of penetration.

The ancient Chinese adapted the position on wedding nights by placing the woman lying back with her hips at the edge of the bed so that her legs hung over the sides, feet touching the floor, the man standing and leaning into her between her parted legs. Presumably the shallow penetration allowed by this missionary variation eased the pain of deflowering.

Deeper penetration can be achieved if the woman opens her legs more widely and bends her knees. She can keep her feet on the bed, hold her legs vertically in the air—or place her feet on his shoulders, which has the effect of tightening the vagina and, some women say, also providing an opportunity for G spot stimulation during intercourse.

She can also wrap her legs around his body. This permits deeper penetration, but does limit movement. Couples with strong PC muscles can use this variation to best advantage.

Best position for: male orgasm. Many men like to switch to the missionary position when they are ready to have an orgasm.

•   *REAR ENTRY.*   Women love this one or they don't. A favorite of the ancient Chinese, the rear-entry position facilitates deep penetration. In the basic version, the woman is on all fours with the man kneeling behind her. She may or may not lower her upper body so that her chest touches the bed. In this position, her vaginal barrel is sloping downward. His thrusting from this angle creates different sensations than she feels in other positions. For example, his penis may feel larger because her vagina is elongated. Or the tighter fit might make her feel that he is entering her more forcefully or more deeply than he can in other positions. And the sensations vary rather dramatically for both partners depending on how fast and hard they thrust and move together. Another plus: Her genitals are easily accessible for either or both of them to stroke.

Why some women don't like it: Rear entry just doesn't sound likable. In America, we refer to this as "doggy style," which connotes negative images. We can blame the French, who first labeled rear-entry positions *en levrette,* or "like a greyhound."

Another reason some women don't like it: They feel dominated by their lovers, who are in position to thrust very deeply without making eye contact. ("Hard fucking without intimacy," as one woman described it.)

Best position for: clitoral, perineum, and G spot stimulation, if the angle is right. Women who do love this position often report stronger orgasms during rear entry than other intercourse positions—again, because the angle can make penetration feel deeper and fuller.

Little embarrassing side effect: Sometimes the vagina in this position sucks in air, which is then dispelled in a noise which sounds suspiciously like a fart and is called by some Englishmen "a betty."

• SPOONS. The French call this one *à la paresseuse,* meaning, "the lazy way." The man faces the woman's back, her buttocks angled against him. He may put one of his legs between hers. In another version, the woman lies half on her side, half on her back, drawing up the leg on which she is lying. The man faces her. Penetration is limited.

Best for: the last trimester of pregnancy; those nights when you're too tired to do it but you want to do it anyway; early mornings when neither of you have brushed your teeth yet; or getting her started when she isn't awake—as long as you know she likes being awakened this way from time to time.

• SITTING. The man may sit in a chair or on the bed, with the woman astride him. He holds on to her buttocks. She has her hands on his shoulders. Or they may sit facing each other in the middle of the bed, legs wrapped around the others bodies. Penetration is shallow. But a woman can make it deeper by leaning backward as he grabs her buttocks and thrusts.

Best for: a man with an extraordinarily large penis.

• STANDING. Having intercourse while standing satisfies a need some of us occasionally have for dramatic, urgent lovemaking. It's a good way to have a quickie in the rest room on a train or plane after you've fondled each other to near orgasm under the blanket in the seats. To achieve insertion, the man will have to squat while the woman lowers herself onto him. If he can hold her, she can wrap her legs around his waist so that he can cup her buttocks while energetically thrusting. Otherwise, she can wrap one leg around his waist and put her weight on the other leg, providing they are similar in height.

Best for: the physically fit in need of a quickie—and women who wear thigh-high stockings and string bikini panties, not panty hose.

The Simultaneous Orgasm Position

Sex therapists have been telling us for years that trying to have an orgasm at the same time your partner does is not realistic. The renewal of interest in simultaneous orgasms, however, has led to the development of two positions.

• *THE CAT.* The Coital Alignment Technique, advocated by American psychotherapist Edward Eichel, is a variation on the old missionary position. Eichel claims the CAT guarantees female orgasm, simultaneous orgasm, and an orgasmic experience superior to anything the couple has ever experienced before. (Many other sex therapists and sexologists vehemently disagree with him.) The woman lies on her back. The man lies on top of her with his full weight so that, with his penis inside her, his pelvis is higher than hers. She wraps her legs around his thighs, resting her ankles on his calves. *They move pelvises only in a steady rhythm, which neither speeds up nor slows down until orgasm is achieved by both.* The woman leads on the upward stroke, pushing the man's pelvis backward while he simultaneously provides a counterpressure on the clitoris with the penile shaft. He leads on the downward stroke, pushing the female pelvis downward while she provides a resistant counter-pressure by pressing her clitoris against the base of his penis.

Best for: women who don't feel comfortable touching their clitorises; men who are determined to "give her an orgasm" without using their hands.

Not good for: women who are considerably smaller than their partners; anyone who likes to move enthusiastically during intercourse.

Comment from a woman: "I tried it and hated the feeling of being squashed under the man's weight. Also, I couldn't stick with it long enough to reach an orgasm." And from a man: "My wife and I tried it and made it work, but weren't overwhelmed with the position. It might be a nice way to end up, a place to finish after a vigorous lovemaking session."

• THE DOG. No, not rear entry. The Dual Orgasm Position was developed as a response to the CAT by British sexologist Diane Poitras using techniques adapted from the *Kama Sutra* and back issues of the magazines *Forum and For Women*. It's a little complicated so I'll break it down into steps:

The couple starts making love in the missionary position, her legs between his widely spaced legs.

With his penis inside her, he slowly rolls onto his side, supporting his upper body weight on his elbow, rolling his partner toward him with the opposite arm.

As she rolls toward him, the woman swings her far leg over his buttocks, bending her knee so that she can hug his body closer to hers with this leg. Her lower leg gives him leverage to thrust into her.

Still supporting his upper body on his arm, he presses her bent leg even closer to his buttocks by holding it near the ankle with his free hand. This gives him more leverage for thrusting into her.

As he thrusts, his uppermost thigh presses firmly against her clitoris, stimulating it.

With his slow thrusts creating the necessary friction on the clitoris, he can time his orgasm to coincide with hers.

An easier variation of the DOG is based on the *Kama Sutra*'s position "splitting the reed." Kneeling, the man leans over the woman, who is lying on her back with her right leg up against his left shoulder and her left leg down to the side, so that he is between her legs. He puts his left hand on her shoulder to steady himself. Once he effects penetration, his thrusts are directed against her raised leg, which increases the pressure on her clitoris.

Comment: "The DOG affords more energetic rolling about than the CAT. But my partner and I did not achieve simultaneous orgasms." And from a man: "These aren't the best positions when you are really excited. They're good for those slow nights when you want to make love but you aren't tearing each other's clothes off. The excitement builds gradually in these positions."

The One Exotic Kama Sutra Position for Any Couple

The X, or Scissors, Position is called "Woman acting the part of the man" in the *Kama Sutra*.

Imagine your bodies forming an X, with the connection at the genitals. The man sits at the edge of the bed with his back straight and one leg outstretched on the bed, the other outstretched toward the floor, or, if he prefers, braced up on a straight-back chair placed by the bed. Her back supported by pillows, the woman sits astride her partner, with both legs braced on his shoulders.

It sounds awkward, but is very comfortable. I had a couple in their sixties, both overweight, test the X. He said, "Very comfortable to hold. And we had the best friction together we've had in a long time." She said, "Great! Because of our tummies, we haven't been getting close enough to each other lately. This worked very well. He was able to play with my breasts while I played with my clitoris. What a revelation!"

GUARANTEED SIMULTANEOUS ORGASM IN ANY POSITION TECHNIQUE

Simultaneous orgasm is great when it happens, which isn't as often as the romantic mythology—reinforced by female faking at the moment of his orgasm—would have us believe. There should be no undue pressure upon a couple to reach orgasm at the same time. As long as both partners are satisfied, who came first is not an issue. However, the emotional satisfaction men and especially women receive from the SO makes it worth the try occasionally. Everything depends on timing—making this a technique most effectively used by couples who know each other's responses well.

Typically, the woman takes longer to reach orgasm, especially during intercourse and even with additional manual stimulation. Time each other's responses during your most familiar pattern of lovemaking. Now you know very nearly how much time it takes each partner to move from full arousal to orgasm. If you have been together a long time, coordinating your timing sequences may not be a lot more difficult than preparing a company meal and having everything ready for the table at the same time.

"My husband says he can tell by a glazed and unfocused look in my eye when I'm on the final countdown to orgasm," reported a devotee of the SO. "We don't begin intercourse until I have reached that stage. He comes within two minutes of being inside me unless we stop and let him pull back to make it last longer."

A man can hold back his own full arousal by devoting himself to arousing her. No fellatio. No intercourse. He should stimulate her orally or manually until she is as close to orgasm as he will be shortly after intercourse begins. If she is multi-orgasmic, of course, the timing is less crucial. And should he be the slower partner, she pays more attention to arousing him than he does her.

$\mathcal{H}$OW OFTEN SHOULD YOU CHANGE POSITIONS?

"I had a lover who changed positions so often, I felt like I was part of the U.S. Olympic team," said Sue. "It got to be distracting. But he did have one really great position that I hadn't done with other men. We sat in the middle of the bed. I liked that the best. I had some great orgasms in the sitting position while he played with my clit. But it was difficult getting him to sit still and do it sometimes.

"On the other hand, I had a lover who wouldn't move from whatever position I started him in. He was like a lump in the bed."

Switch positions too often and you can feel like you're playing sexual musical chairs. The pace is too frenetic. On the other hand, you don't want to stay in one position so long that someone gets a muscle cramp.

Dr. Kothari said, "Change positions when you need to change the genital stimulation. Perhaps he needs to pull back to keep from ejaculating or thrust harder so he can ejaculate. Perhaps she needs to have repeated stimulation to reach orgasm and so he needs to stay in place to keep giving her the same stimulation until she is satisfied. Don't change positions because you think it will look pretty in the mirror or will impress your partner with your physical dexterity."

Does he think some positions are better than others?

"What is better depends on what you want at the time," he said. "The face-to-face positions, female superior and missionary, are greatly satisfying to the senses and the emotions. All five sensory organs of both partners come into contact with each other. The tongues, ears, eyes, mouths, noses, and all the skin are in touch.

"Sometimes couples want other things. The rear entry is very exciting for the man and the woman. It is incomparable for thrusting. Everything depends on the couple's need at the moment."

Chapter Twelve

THRUSTING

I love intercourse and so does my wife," Jonathan said. "She likes me to enter her with a deep thrust or two, then switch to light playful strokes for a while. Sometimes we both want it hard and fast and sometimes slow, deep thrusting. If I pull back and angle my penis high against the top of her vaginal opening, I make her clitoral hood move, stimulating her little bud. I can make her come this way. She says it feels like I am fucking her clitoris.

"We've found we can make intercourse last a long time by varying the speed, depth, and angle of the thrust and by moving from one position to another. We like to switch positions without losing the genital contact. She has strong muscles so she can hold me inside her while we roll over, even if I'm going a little soft.

"She says she loves feeling me inside her as much as I love being there."

Though there is certainly more to "sex" than intercourse, many, if not most, men and women find that act more deeply satisfying on both a physical and emotional level than any other form of lovemaking. We want and need to connect with each other in this special way. Would a heterosexual sexual relationship be complete without intercourse?

There's more to intercourse than getting into position. Yet little has been said about the importance of thrusting techniques in contemporary sex-advice books. The style, angle, and depth of penetration change the experience. If you grind your hips close together, you feel your partner in a different way than when you each pull hips back and push forcefully—or softly—against each other. "Coital dynamics," or the art of thrusting, changes everything.

Taoist master Mantak Chia has taught workshops for men in many different cities, including San Francisco, Amsterdam, Tokyo, and Berlin. Men of all ages, gay and straight, take his classes. Their occupations run the gamut from doctors, businessmen, and academics to cooks, garment workers, mass transit engineers. I caught up with him in Amsterdam. He was instructing students on the fine art of thrusting at the New Ancient Sex Academy, where visiting lecturers teach the esoteric philosophies and techniques of Tantric and Taoist sex. Steeped in both disciplines at an early age, Chia was raised near a Buddhist temple in Thailand and "hung out with monks." Later he studied under Taoist teachers.

We met in the historic center of the city at an outdoor café close to the red-light district, where prostitution has flourished since the thirteenth century. In this oldest part of the city, prostitutes sit in lighted windows at street level, advertising their availability, as much a part of the fabric of Amsterdam as the tree-lined canals, the tulips, the Rembrandts, and the van Goghs. In the fabled city of open minds, Chia explained the difference between the Tantric (from India and Tibet) and Taoist (from China) approaches to sex.

"The Taoist path and the Tantric path differ mainly in their language and in the practical yogic methods taught to achieve the same union of mind, body, and spirit. Both fully accept the mastery of one's sexuality as not only a legitimate but necessary means to attain the highest enlightenment possible in the body. Both subscribe to the importance of semen retention.

"Only the Taoists do not personify the subtle energies with a pantheon of divine beings. So I would say that the Tantra is for someone who is more interested in the religious archetypes—the

gods and goddesses, the Bodisattvas and demons—and their elaborate secret rituals, initiations, and invocations using mantra."

In researching this book, I attended some workshops, seminars,
and retreats that incorporated sex techniques into a program of spiritual enlightenment. Mantak Chia is right when he says that Tantric
sex enthusiasts are fond of elaborate and secret rituals. Remember,
Tantric has its roots in the Hindu concept of sacred sexuality. In a
weekend dedicated to "sex magic," a self-styled guru in Portland,
Oregon, instructed participants to write their life wishes—from
more money to better sex—on paper and put them under the mattress. Making love atop your wish list, while sending your same
thoughts skyward "in mental pink balloons" was part of his program
for getting what you want out of life through sex. This is fairly
ephemeral stuff for the average Westerner. (Was I disappointed! I had
a different idea of what "sex magic" would be.) Buried in the workshop lesson plan was some good advice on how to make intercourse
last longer, though no Tantric or Taoist instructor ever makes that
the obvious point of the exercise.

For our purposes: Taoists take the concept of semen retention further than Tantrics do. They have more techniques for delaying ejaculation. And Tantrics, who worship the male and female genitalia, have
more advice on how to make oral love and more little tricks for deep-
ening the emotional connection between couples while making love.

"Many men believe the best way to excite a woman is deeply
thrusting," Chia said. "They think the regular pumping rhythm of
deep strokes is the only way. Then they are surprised when they
ejaculate too soon."

Chia teaches men how to perform intercourse for longer periods of time by varying the pattern of thrusting. Varied genital movements during intercourse create different kinds and degrees of
stimulation. The hard, deep, and regular thrusting pattern considered the ideal in Western culture leads to ejaculation in minutes, if
not seconds. Men can prolong intercourse by periodically with-
drawing while continuing to stimulate their partner manually or
orally. But they can also prolong intercourse without withdrawal—

or through partial withdrawal—if they change the coital dynamics. In addition to lasting longer, they can give themselves and their partners a far more varied genital experience. Prolonging intercourse is a worthy goal for most couples.

Women love thrusting, too. Even women who rarely reach orgasm during intercourse alone can't imagine lovemaking without it.

"I like penetration," said Candy, who typically has her orgasm via cunnilingus or manual stimulation. "I feel totally fulfilled as a woman during intercourse. I love the other parts of lovemaking, but intercourse is still the best. There is nothing like the sensation of having a man inside of you, having a man come inside of you.

"Penetration is physically and psychologically satisfying for me. I can have an orgasm during intercourse if I use my hand. Sometimes I do and sometimes I just want to experience him inside me and have my orgasm another way."

MALE COITAL DYNAMICS

"A good lover uses different methods of thrusting to stimulate different areas of the female genitalia," Chia says. "The clitoral area is extremely sensitive, as is the cervix in some women. The front wall of the vagina is more sensitive to friction and pressure than the back wall in most women. The rim of the vagina is not sensitive. The man must use his shaft to best advantage in each area.

"A favorite position with the ancient eroticists was Wild Horses Leaping [the missionary position with the woman's knees bent and feet on man's shoulders, see page 157] because the woman could not move even her sexual muscles and the man was able to stimulate her clitoris with his stalk. He entered her so that the underside of his shaft pressed against the back wall of the vagina and he could use the head to massage the front of her vagina."

I am able to flex my PC muscles in this position. And the other women I consulted said they could, too. Perhaps he meant to say that women don't flex as easily in the pose of Wild Horses Leaping.

"I can flex them in that position," one woman said. "If I don't, I can sometimes get an orgasm from the vaginal stimulation alone. It depends on how aroused I was before we settled into this position."

And another woman said, "It's satisfying, either way, whether I flex or I don't. Sometimes you need to be still to feel what his penis can do for you."

In any position, Chia recommends thrusting techniques that vary depth and speed of movement. His students' success with the techniques depends on how long they have studied Taoist methods and how far they want to take the training. It ranges from some who are content to extend intercourse by several minutes to half an hour to others who push the training further and achieve extended orgasms, multiples orgasms, and orgasms without ejaculation.

Hans, a thirty-five-year-old journalist, told me he had taken two workshops with Mantak Chia, one approximately a year prior to this current one.

"I wanted some control over the ejaculatory process," he said. "Every man wants to be a better lover. To me, a good lover has some control over when he ejaculates in order that he may pleasure his partner and himself for a longer period of time before ejaculating. I have never been one to stop making love with my own orgasm. I would make love to my partner for as long as she wished and help her to achieve however many orgasms she desired or could have.

"Still, you know both partners feel differently about the love-making after the man had his orgasm. Some of the intensity is gone, for the woman as well. Some women feel a little embarrassed about continuing, no matter how much you reassure them. I wanted to last longer. I had heard from a friend about the Taoist training and I thought I should try it. I saw immediate improvement using the thrusting techniques. By changing the dynamics, I was able to make intercourse last twice as long, up to fifteen minutes.

"Now, I am greedy, you know. I am going for more. I wasn't paying as much attention to all the training the first time because my mind couldn't get around the concepts. Now I think they are possible and I am back for more."

The "Eight Slow, Two Fast" Thrusting Method

• The man should exhale on the outward strokes and inhale on the inward strokes. The depth of penetration varies in the slow strokes from shallow to deep. But the two fast strokes are deep. (Couples can use any intercourse position preferred for these exercises.)

My lover and I found it more fun to vary the speed and depth of the strokes *without* counting. His reaction to the counting: "I feel like men must have felt when they were told to delay orgasm until the woman had come during intercourse by thinking of baseball statistics." And the other three couples who tried this method had similar experiences. Only one managed to keep the count for several minutes. He said, "Intercourse does last longer. Maybe if you do this for a while, it will become habit and you won't have to count."

The "Nine Shallow, One Deep" Thrusting Method

• The number nine is of great importance in Taoist thinking because it is considered to hold a powerful "yang," or male, energy. In the nine shallow thrusts method, the penis enters only two or three inches into the vagina to stimulate the G spot (again, presuming she thinks she has one) and create a vacuum in the vagina. The deep thrust forces the air out of the vagina, making the penis feel more closely held. The man should not withdraw completely at any point because that would break the vacuum seal. After nine sets of nine shallow, one deep, vary the thrusting pattern.

My lover and I lost track of the count after the first set, but did find that alternating several shallow thrusts with a deep one varied the stimulation for both of us and helped him delay ejaculation. I found it more exciting once we did lose the count, because the deep thrust came as a surprise. Another couple said, "We lost track right away, but we did vary the thrusts, which made intercourse last longer and feel better. We didn't notice that vacuum-seal effect. I hadn't realized that I wasn't putting much variety in the thrusting until we got involved in this little experiment."

And a woman said, "It's amazing how much difference one small change makes. We kept track of the counts until we were both close to orgasm. It was intense. Intercourse lasted longer—and so, we believe, did orgasm."

Japanese Variation: The Set of Nines

• The man enters the woman and performs nine shallow thrusts. He withdraws, pauses, enters, and performs eight shallow thrusts, followed by one deep thrust. Again he withdraws, enters, performs seven shallow thrusts, and then two deep. The set continues in this manner until he takes nine deep strokes—which is supposed to bring her to orgasm.

This was much nicer. My partner and I still lost count. So did three other couples who nevertheless found the effort worth doing. One couple kept the count all the way through the nine deep strokes. "I did reach orgasm," she said, "but I was manipulating my clit as I always do. I didn't start until the last set so that the orgasm began when he was finishing the nine deep strokes."

The Corkscrew

• In this case, the missionary position is the best but not only possible alternative. The man, his weight supported on his arms, turns his body slightly to the right, then the left while thrusting.

The panel of testers highly recommends this move—in either the missionary or rear-entry position. A woman said, "When performed in the rear-entry position, the corkscrew brought me to a deep, shuddering orgasm. This surprised both of us." One man said, "I had a little trouble getting the motion to be smooth and fluid at first. But once I got over that—and over feeling silly about doing it—we both liked the sensations. At first, these exercises might make you laugh. It's rather amusing to count your strokes. Persevere, we say. Soon the laughter turns into panting."

FEMALE COITAL DYNAMICS

"I can exert a great deal of control over the thrusting during intercourse by how I angle my body," said Mindy, who was part of my coital dynamics testing group. "The perception is that men thrust and women receive, but that isn't true. I can get his penis to come in at a different angle by moving my pelvis. And I can control the speed by matching or not matching his thrusts. If I want him to slow down, I slow down. He follows my lead as often as I do his, even if he is the one on top."

A woman can change coital dynamics most easily in the female-superior position because she controls the angle and depth of penetration and the speed of thrusting. But she can get a different sensation in almost any position simply by shifting her body so that the penis comes into the vagina at a different angle. (This leaves out the CAT.)

The following techniques are recommended by Chia, who also teaches classes in female coital dynamics, along with his wife, Maneewan. The female students, like their male counterparts, represent all ages and come from various occupations, including teaching, nursing, business, law, and waitressing. Though this group was largely heterosexual, many lesbian women practice Tantric sex, too.

The Oval Track

• Typically the woman moves up and down while riding in the female-superior position. She can vary that movement with the oval track. During the downward movement onto his penis, if she leans slightly forward and pushes her pubis slightly to the back, her clitoral area can be stimulated by his shaft. During the upward movement, if she leans slightly backward and pushes her pubis slightly forward, her front vaginal wall, and the G spot, may be stimulated by the head of the penis.

Comment: Four-star gyration. "This move could make a G spot believer out of me," said a woman who tested it. "Nothing has ever persuaded me to think I had one of those spots before I tried the oval track. You never know. It just proves we have more areas of erotic sensitivity than we realize."

The Pause

• In any position, at the moment of his deepest penetration, grasp his buttocks and hold him tightly, prolonging the moment of contact.

This is even better if you grasp his penis tightly with your PC muscles at the same time you're holding his buttocks. One woman said, "This is something I'v always done naturally. When I'm really into the experience, I lock my eyes with his as I'm clasping him hard into me. Intense feelings come to the surface when you make love this way."

The PC Flex

• The woman times the flexing of her PC muscles with her partner's thrusting. She relaxes her muscles until his penis is inside her vagina. Then she constricts the muscles. The flex varies in intensity and duration.

Flexing can bring on an orgasm quickly for a woman with strong PC muscles, which makes it a good thing to do if you want to have an orgasm via intercourse alone. A man whose partner frequently employs the PC flex said, "I enjoy lovemaking more with Kay than with any woman I've ever known—largely because of the way she grabs my penis with her love muscles. She really wants me. She's a totally active partner. I never worry about losing an erection with her. I never worry about anything to do with performance when I'm with her."

The Butterfly Quiver

•   While the French refer to it as *pompoir,* the ancient Chinese called this variation on the PC flex the Butterfly Quiver. It was a specialty of priestesses and renowned courtesans. The woman flexes her PC muscles in a continuous pattern of tightening and releasing, which replicates the pulsating of butterfly wings, when her lover is near ejaculation. Most effective when he does not thrust too vigorously and leaves the movement largely to her. If she has good muscles, it will feel as if the ejaculate is being pulled from his body.

This is very satisfying for both partners. I found this highly arousing. Another woman said: "He had a tremendous orgasm when I did the Butterfly Quiver on him. I didn't warn him in advance. Afterward he said, 'My God, what was that? My God, that was wonderful!' When I continued to hold his penis with my PC muscles after ejaculation, he was able to sustain his erection. He thinks I'm a goddess."

Part 6

ORGASMS

Chapter Thirteen

THE BIGGER, WILDER O

W e sat in a circle, did various breathing exercises, and chanted in unison to 'evoke the ancient spirits,'" Kate said. "Bill and I rolled our eyes at each other. What had we gotten ourselves into?

"Jwala prattled on about chakras and enlightened energy and rejuvenating sex, and I was thinking, 'Well, that's five hundred dollars wasted.'

"She went around the circle and asked us each to make a prayer statement of purpose on why we were there and what we had to accomplish. Bill said he prayed he would make an extra five hundred in commissions the next week to cover this. There was some tittering in response, but we were definitely the class A skeptics of the crowd.

"We searched the eyes of each person in the circle, chanted some more, did some exercises, and finally got into a mudra, a position with your partner for circulating sexual energy. The first mudra was crown to crown. Bill and I lay on the carpeted floor with our heads touching for fifteen minutes while soft Eastern music played, the kind of music he hates to hear in Indian restaurants. She told us to breathe deeply and expand our realizations of self.

"More mudras. Toes to forehead. Heart to foot to hand. Finally we were in a sitting mudra, both of us facing each other with me on top, our legs wrapped around each other, right hand at back of partner's neck, left hand on partner's tailbone.

"Bill's hands began to work a kind of magic on my body. He pressed his palm firmly at the base of my spine, sliding it up my back and neck, and down again, back up, as Jwala directed and grabbed a handful of my hair and tugging it gently.

"'Feel the sexual energy moving up from the lower genital chakra,' she said. Incredibly I did feel the energy moving, chakra or no chakra. I had never felt so aroused. He kept rubbing my back as he inserted his penis inside my vagina. We rocked slowly together, more rocking than thrusting, the excitement building, until we were rocking and rolling, him thrusting joyously into me, never mind the mudra, and I came in a big wild explosion."

Five couples attended Jwala's Tantric workshop that Friday evening in a secluded home in suburban Philadelphia. One of a handful of worldwide Tantric teachers, Jwala, in her early forties, is a pretty brunette of Irish, not Indian, descent, who has been studying Tantra since she was a teenager. She carries two large trunks filled with incense, candles, cassette tapes, lengths of colorful cloth, and assorted "magic" items, such as crystals and charms, all over the world. The workshops rarely end in the participants having intercourse as this one did.

In fact, at most Tantric workshops, the couples do not remove their clothing. Positions are demonstrated by the fully clothed teachers, sometimes using visual aides such as videos, dolls, and drawings. And participants go back to their rooms and practice what they have been told to do.

Kate and two other women said they had bigger, wilder orgasms that night than they typically had. Was it magic?

THE ORGASM

"Orgasm is the most intensely pleasurable sensation I've ever experienced, whether it's a brief ejaculation or a full body rush," a man I interviewed said, describing his orgasm.

"Sometimes an orgasm feels concentrated in my genitals and sometimes it is diffuse, but it is always an incredible release, an explosion of pleasure that leaves little concentric circles rippling happily in its wake," a woman said, describing her orgasm.

Most of us think orgasms are about as good as it gets on the pleasure scale. Yet, some anxiety frequently surrounds the word *orgasm*. Men worry about coming "too soon," while women worry about "taking too long." The word has its roots in two Greek words: *orgasmos,* meaning "to grow ripe, swell, and be lustful," and *orge,* meaning "impulse." No worry in either word.

In 1940 Wilhelm Reich in his groundbreaking book, *The Function of the Orgasm,* broadened the definition of orgasm beyond the genitals. He was the first sexologist to say that a person's emotional health was related to his or her capacity to experience orgasm. Reich thought orgasm was a whole-body event—a belief he shared with the Eastern sexologists, and one that was largely ignored by Western authorities on the subject.

Her Orgasm

When a woman is aroused, blood flow increases to the vagina, swelling the inner and outer lips and the clitoris and causing lubrication. With enough intense physical and psychological stimulation, she will reach climax, during which the vagina, sphincter, and uterus contract simultaneously, and the blood congested in the vaginal area suddenly rushes back to the rest of the body.

The entire explosion, or set of contractions, generally lasts a mere three to twenty seconds, with intervals of less than a second between the first three to six contractions. Some women experience single orgasms lasting a minute or more, and some women feel post-orgasmic contractions, particularly in the uterus, up to twenty-four hours later. And some women do feel the orgasm radiating throughout their bodies.

The debate over whether or not women have clitoral or vaginal orgasms or both still continues. Sigmund Freud distinguished clitoral from vaginal orgasm and labeled the former "immature" and "neurotic." The adolescent girl experienced clitoral orgasm during masturbation. Once she became sexually active with a partner, she switched to vaginal orgasms—or so thought Freud, who didn't know much about female anatomy.

In 1953 Alfred Kinsey in his landmark study, *Sexual Behavior in the Human Female,* said all female orgasms were achieved by clitoral stimulation, either direct or indirect. His findings were endorsed a decade later by pioneer sex researchers William Masters and Virginia Johnson, who isolated the orgasm in the lab and measured and quantified the process. The clitoral orgasm theory became the prevailing opinion among sex therapists until 1980, when Beverly Whipple and John Perry claimed their research proved the existence of the G spot and therefore put the female orgasm back inside the vagina.

Their findings have never been accepted by the majority of Western sexologists. The late Helen Singer Kaplan, Ph.D., a pioneer in the field of sex therapy and founder of the country's first clinic for sexual disorders, insisted that 75 percent of women do not reach orgasm during intercourse without some kind of direct clitoral stimulation. And studies conducted by researchers and reported upon in scientific journals consistently report that 60 to 75 percent of women are unable to reach orgasm without clitoral stimulation. Furthermore, less than 10 percent of women report discovering the elusive G spot in both popular magazine surveys and research conducted by university scientists. Still, there's nothing wrong with the G spot theory as long as the theorists promote the spot as an additional pleasure zone, not the route by which all women *should* be orgasmic. The myth of the mature vaginal orgasm should have been buried with Freud.

His Orgasm

According to the prevailing opinion of Western sex therapists, male orgasm and ejaculation are the same thing. Some sexologists, however, share the Eastern belief that male orgasm, like female, is a psycho-physical experience that in addition, unlike female, typically includes ejaculation, but not always. These sexologists separate the pleasurable sensations of the rhythmic contractions resulting from the release of tension from the expulsion of semen. In either case, following the engorgement of blood vessels, which takes place during arousal, the male experiences contractions of the penis and surrounding genital area as pleasurable sensations similar in timing sequence and length to female orgasm.

Can men have multiples? Again, sexologists do not agree. Those who believe orgasm and ejaculation are separate claim a man can have multiple climaxes, just as a woman can. If the male orgasm is defined in ejaculatory terms, however, few men are able to ejaculate more than once within a brief span of time, making the male multiple rare.

How IMPORTANT IS ORGASM?

"If I hadn't experienced that intense orgasm at Jwala's workshop, I would have thought we'd wasted our five hundred dollars," said Kate. "But I did and we didn't."

That's how important orgasm is.

Americans have been accused of being too goal-oriented about sex. When we say *sex,* we mean *intercourse*—and we don't expect to roll over afterward feeling less than sated. Some other cultures approach sex in a more languid and sensual way. Sex doesn't always have to include intercourse. The Eastern arts focus on both the spiritual and physical aspects of sex.

The Indian guru Bhagwan Shree Rajneesh, who brought the cult of Tantra to the United States, has been frequently quoted as saying that "real Tantra is not technique, but love, not head-oriented, but a relaxation into the heart." He says that "ordinary sexual orgasm looks like madness," while Tantra is "a source of pure bliss." If that philosophy appeals to you, there are many books about the spiritual aspects of Eastern sexology. But they don't all agree with the Bhagwan's interpretation.

One school of Tantric thought teaches that an orgasm a day keeps the doctor away. I chose to cast my lot with those thinkers and focus solely on techniques that could be adapted for the average Western couple who want to give themselves and each other more pleasure—and for better or worse, more pleasure does mean bigger, wilder orgasms to most of us. That particular form of madness *is* bliss.

$\mathcal{W}$HAT ARE THE COMPONENTS OF THE BIGGER, WILDER O?

Why did Kate and two other women have bigger, wilder orgasms at Jwala's workshop than they typically had or had expected to have?

And, equally important, why did their partners find the experience not quite *that* satisfying?

Sexual satisfaction is a blend of physical, psychological, and emotional factors. In the workshop setting the women found what they needed: excitement of a new setting and situation, slow buildup of sexual tension beginning with nongenital touching, deep emotional contact with their partners through the eye lock, and an intercourse position that stimulated the clitoris. The men, on the other hand, didn't get quite enough of what they needed: variety in coital dynamics.

Bill said, "I found the experience enjoyable, but not mind-blowing. For me, that came later when Kate and I made love using the stroking and the eye lock and the position through her first orgasm, then switching to more conventional positions for me. I had also by that time perfected some of the [Taoist] techniques for delaying orgasm so that mine was as intense as hers."

When Bill and Kate repeated the workshop exercises at home with the changes made to accommodate his needs, they both had "tremendous" orgasms. Obviously, you can have "tremendous" orgasms under other circumstances and in other positions than the method described below. But try this. You may be surprised.

$\mathcal{H}$OW TO HAVE ONE VERSION OF THE BIGGER, WILDER ORGASM

The Setting

• This is not going to be a quickie. Allow plenty of time for lovemaking. Light candles, burn incense, arrange fresh flowers in vases on the bedside tables, play soft music.

The Build-up

• Lie in each other's arms. Stroke and caress and fondle each part of the other's body, except the genitals. Devote as much time to this as necessary to reach the point where you are aching to touch each other.

The Eye Lock

• Look deeply into each other's eyes as you are caressing. Hold the look. Do this more than once. You probably won't realize how little you do look into each other's eyes during lovemaking until you practice the eye lock.

Assume the Yubyam Position

• Sit in the center of the bed facing each other. Wrap your legs around each other so that she is "sitting" on his legs. Place your right hand at the back of your partner's neck, your left hand on partner's tailbone.

• Each press your palm firmly at the base of your partner's spine. Slide your hand up his or her back to the back of the neck, and then to the top of the head. Imagine you are channeling sexual energy up through the body, warming the body from genitals through heart through head. Repeat the stroke over and over again until you are both feeling very aroused.

• Insert his penis into her vagina so that the shaft exerts as much indirect pressure as possible on her clitoris. Rock slowly together as you rub each other's back and perform the eye lock.

• After her orgasm, make love in other positions, varying the speed, thrust, and angle of thrusting to prolong his excitation phase as long as possible.

DELAYING HIS ORGASM

"When I have an orgasm too soon after starting intercourse now, I feel cheated," Bill said. "It's a little orgasm, like a squirt, compared to what I can have when I delay."

How can you delay male orgasm? Technique, technique, technique.

Some people advise wearing a cock ring, a metal, latex, or leather ring placed around the base of the penis. This can heighten sensation and delay orgasm and even, in some men, create a larger

erection. However, cock rings can bruise. They can also be dangerous if left on for longer than twenty to thirty minutes because they
work by restricting the flow of blood out of the penis.

And some people will tell you that passion and enthusiasm are
everything. Inevitably they are the men who squeeze one's breasts
like oranges being juiced, the women who nick your manhood with
their teeth. They are hasty lovers. Without discounting the importance of passion and enthusiasm, technique counts.

Technique in loveplay is invaluable in bridging the sex gap between the genders. There are individual exceptions, but in general
men are at their biological sexual peak between the ages of sixteen
and twenty, while women peak much later, between thirty and forty.
A man is normally more easily aroused than his female partner, who
requires longer and more varied forms of manual or oral stimulation
for arousal and orgasm. A certain level of skill is required to bring
both partners to a bigger, wilder orgasmic conclusion.

To arouse his partner while delaying his own ejaculation, a man
must have some techniques at his disposal.

The Delay Techniques

Masters and Johnson modeled the squeeze technique, squeezing
the head of the penis to retard ejaculation, on these more elegant
Taoist exercises.

- *THE THREE-FINGER METHOD.* Practiced in China
for five thousand years, this technique is simple and, according to Mantak Chia, "considerably effective." (It is also
much like the perineum massage. Only in this method, you
use three curved fingers to apply pressure to one spot on the
perineum at the point of ejaculatory inevitability, rather
than massaging the whole area, which does create a different result.) Locate the pressure point mid-perineum, the
place between the anus and the scrotum. "Use the three

longest fingers to the right hand to apply pressure—not too light and not too hard—to the perineum point as soon as you feel the inevitability of orgasm." The fingers should be curved slightly.

The men who tested this reported that it does indeed work to delay orgasm. One man advised, "Practice during masturbation because finding the exact spot and getting the pressure just right is a little tricky. And keeping the fingers curved makes a difference though I couldn't tell you why." And Bill said, "My orgasm is definitely stronger now that I frequently practice the three-finger method."

• *THE BIG DRAW.* This technique requires strong PC muscles. "When you perfect it," Chia said, "you won't need to use the three fingers anymore." When you feel ejaculation is imminent, stop thrusting. Pull back to approximately one inch of penetration, but do not entirely withdraw. Flex the PC muscles and hold to a count of nine. Or you may wish to try flexing nine times in rapid succession instead of holding the count. Resume thrusting with shallow strokes.

My panel of men said this is more difficult to perform than the three-finger technique. One man said, "You really need to tell your partner what you're doing and get her to hold back with you. This isn't going to work if she's ready to have an orgasm. At that point, she wants you to thrust and she'd rather you ejaculate than hold back."

• *ALTERNATING STIMULI.* If you are highly aroused but not on the verge of ejaculation, stop thrusting and make love to your partner manually or orally. By alternating intercourse with other forms of lovemaking, most men can make the experience last longer. In sex therapy, this is sometimes referred to as the "stop–start technique."

A man said, "The mistake men make is in assuming that once you've started intercourse, you should keep on fucking until you both have orgasms. Once you stop drawing the line between intercourse and foreplay, you can make love longer."

And from a woman whose husband says she is adept at "delaying tactics": "I know it's out of favor, but the old Masters and Johnson squeeze technique does work if you do it at the right time. When you sense he is near the point of ejaculation, maneuver your hand so that you can press the ridge surrounding the head of his penis between two fingers for a few seconds. Then resume stimulation in an altered position. My husband likes me to do this three or four times during intercourse so he can last longer and also have a stronger orgasm when he does come."

• *THE TENDER TUG.* Encircle your partner's scrotum with thumb and fingers as he nears ejaculation. Squeeze firmly and pull down lightly. Hold for several seconds. This should delay his orgasm. However, if you squeeze *too* firmly or pull down *too* hard, you will cause pain.

My panel of testers found this a less reliable delaying tactic than the others because it depended on their communicating to their partners that ejaculation was imminent. One man said, "By the time I let her know and she got her hand in place, it was all over." Another said, "This took some coordinating for my wife and me, but it did work."

OTHER VERSIONS OF THE BIGGER, WILDER O

"The biggest orgasms I have are during masturbation," a married woman in her thirties said. "I would never tell my husband that. Lovemaking is wonderful and special. I do have orgasms. But the huge explosions that go on and on only happen during masturbation."

It is not unusual for people to report stronger orgasms during masturbation than lovemaking, which makes mutual masturbation an attractive way of sharing yourself with your partner (see page 67). Nor is it unusual for both men and women to experience their orgasms as "stronger" or "better" when the lovemaking has been particularly emotional.

A man, also married and in his thirties, said, "The most incredible orgasm I ever had was the night my wife and I made love after she got a positive reading from a home pregnancy test. I felt so intensely close to her that all my senses were heightened. We didn't do anything wild or different when we made love, but the feelings were just out of control. You can't predict an experience like that one."

Other people described first-time experiences with their partners, lovemaking after a separation or a prolonged misunderstanding, first lovemaking after childbirth, and similar "special" circumstances. Obviously, the challenge for lovers lies in creating the climate of emotional intensity that favors a bigger, wilder orgasm—and then employing the techniques to make it happen. And, no, it isn't going to happen every time no matter what you do.

*F*EMALE EJACULATION

Female ejaculation isn't exactly a technique. Some devotees of goddess cults claim that every woman can learn to ejaculate during orgasm. They are a minority opinion. A more common response would be: Women—*ejaculate?*

"I was forty before I had a partner who ejaculated," said Jeff, "and I thought she was just peeing all over me."

Female ejaculation is dismissed by Western sex experts as either a myth or a gush of fluid composed of urine and copious vaginal secretions. There is no question that whatever this fluid that some women ejaculate, or squirt, upon orgasm is, it isn't the female equivalent of seminal fluid. The ancients recognized that fact. Hippocrates set forth a "two semen" theory in which he stated that both men and women ejaculate.

Men ejaculate sperm from the testicles via tubes that go through the prostate gland, where it mixes with prostatic fluid. Women do not have a prostate, but in some women there is a collection of several masses of tissue strung out along the urinary tract, referred to as the skeen gland. Medical researcher Josephine Lowndes Sevely claims that in some women this gland produces a fluid that is neither urine nor vaginal secretions.

"I do on occasion ejaculate or squirt or shoot a stream of fluid," one woman said, "but I have never captured the liquid and taken it to a lab for analysis. It neither smells nor tastes like urine. And in truth it feels more like a gush of fluid coming from deep inside. I can anticipate when it's going to happen because on those occasions I am wetter than normal—and normal is *wet*."

Some women are terribly embarrassed about being ejaculators. If you are a man, don't ask her if she peed on you.

Chapter Fourteen

MULTIPLE ORGASMS

On a beautiful Saturday afternoon in Santa Barbara, California, Lisa described her experience with multiple orgasms to a group of women who had paid $250 each for an afternoon workshop on the subject.

"I feel the first of the many orgasms I have during a typical love-making session begin beneath the tip of my partner's tongue as he is licking the sides of my clitoris," she said. "The first one is always from oral stimulation. And I can literally feel him pulling it out of me with the tip of his tongue. First he coaxes it, teases it, with light little flicks, then he pulls it out with long, slow strokes.

"I keep my eyes closed for the first one so I can concentrate on nothing but the feelings in my clit and my fingers entwined in his hair, so I can pull him into me when I need to feel him harder. Riding his tongue, I come in what feels like a shower of sparks. Then, I gyrate my hips so that his mouth slowly makes wide circles around the exquisitely tender clitoris until I am ready to ride him again.

"This time I open my eyes and watch him, because nothing can distract me, and watching him lick and suck me adds to the excitement now. After another orgasm or two, I want him to fuck me for a while, until I come again by touching myself. Then we switch positions. Sometimes he lies on his side and stimulates me with his hand until I come and come again and again.

"I like to have the last one as close to his ejaculation as I can manage it."

The seven women—all blond in one shade or another and apparently in their thirties—were transfixed. The notebooks came out later when Lisa broke down the process into steps. An attractive woman in her late thirties, Lisa—who does not use a last name, like Madonna—is not a therapist. An "incredibly multi-orgasmic woman," she was inspired by the work of therapist Gina Ogden, Ph.D., the author of *Women Who Love Sex,* to teach her techniques for achieving multiple orgasms to other women.

"Most of the women who take the workshop report back to me that they are now able to have multiples on a fairly regular basis," Lisa said. "These are women who are already orgasmic. We aren't starting from square one. I make sure of that before they take the workshop. If they aren't orgasmic, they need a different kind of instruction than I can provide. And they don't need the pressure of trying to go from zero to many overnight."

Her students receive two hours of instruction on a Saturday afternoon and two more hours the following Sunday afternoon.

"That gives them Saturday night to practice," she said. "When they come back on Sunday, they have more specific questions. And through sharing their experiences, they help each other."

Most classes, she assured me, were not this uniform in age and blondness. ("Well, this is So. Cal.," she said, laughing. "Probably seventy percent of the women are blondes.) Typically six to twelve women sign up for the workshop. The majority are married, living with someone, or "significantly involved." ("You want those multiples more when you're with a regular partner," she said. "It means so much to men.") The age range is from the twenties through late forties.

"I don't get many women older than fifty, which could be because women know how to do it by that age—or else they don't care," she said. "The youngest women, in their early to mid-twenties, have the most trouble making it happen. I tell them to relax into the idea of multiples. Women get more comfortable with their sexuality and become more orgasmic as they move into their thirties.

"If it isn't happening for them in their twenties, I tell them to file their notes away in a folder marked, 'Open on my thirtieth birthday.'"

Lisa's advice is on target. Numerous research studies have shown that women do become more easily orgasmic as they move into their thirties and beyond.

On Sunday afternoon, when the group met for the second time, four out of seven reported success in achieving multiples. The remaining three were confident they would break through the single-orgasm barrier in a relatively short time.

"He was performing cunnilingus on me and I felt him hit the right spot," a woman said. "I held his head there because I just knew this time I would go from one orgasm to another if I kept him there. In the past, I always pulled back after the orgasm and then we made love and he had his and that was that. Last night I had several orgasms orally and then surprised myself by coming again during intercourse."

FEMALE MULTIPLES

Lisa is the type of woman most women envy. She rarely has just one orgasm. Physiologically, all women are capable of having multiple orgasms, though probably less than 50 percent do. Unlike men, women don't need a refractory period to "recover" from one orgasm in order to have another. If a woman wants to have multiples, she can. There are four types of multiples.

- COMPOUNDED SINGLE ORGASMS. Each orgasm is distinct, separated by sufficient time so that prior arousal and tension have substantially resolved between orgasms.

- SEQUENTIAL MULTIPLES. Orgasms are fairly close together—anywhere from two to ten minutes apart—with little interruption in sexual stimulation or level of arousal.

- SERIAL MULTIPLES. Orgasms are separated by seconds, or up to two or three minutes, with no, or barely any, interruption in stimulation or diminishment of arousal.

- BLENDED MULTIPLES. A mix of two or more of the above types. Very often women who are multiply orgasmic experience more than one type of multiple orgasm during a lovemaking session.

WHAT CAN A WOMAN DO TO ENCOURAGE MULTIPLE ORGASMS?

Focus. A woman must be focused on her pleasure to achieve multiples. Mental attitude is critical. She isn't likely to have more than one if she's feeling stressed or angry or not sexy. Shutting out intrusive thoughts—sometimes even the thought of your partner's pleasure—also helps.

"That's why I close my eyes for the first orgasm," Lisa said. "To get myself going on that high, I need to be totally focused on my own pleasure with no distractions. Maybe that sounds selfish, but it isn't. When you give a man the gift of your multiple orgasms, you give him something very special. Besides, that complete focus on me is only necessary for the first one. After that, I am more open to him than I am at any other time."

"I have multiple orgasms fairly easily, but I don't have them if I'm not in the mood," said Alicia. "The mood is less determined by anything my partner does than men generally care to believe. I have to be in the right psychological place to open myself up to that much pleasure. On a rare occasion my lover might be able to take me there in spite of myself—but that's rare. It starts right in my head."

Discard Old Attitudes.   A woman will probably never have multiples if she subscribes to these two old-fashioned ideas about sex: You shouldn't have to touch yourself during lovemaking. The lovemaking ends with his ejaculation.

"For years, I thought I had to rush to have an orgasm before the man had his," Cynthia said. "That was the number I was doing on myself, not the fault of the men I'd known. They wanted to continue stimulating me after they came. I was too embarrassed to go on. What was wrong with me?

"I finally loosened up one night in Spain with a man I'd met on a business trip. We'd made love in the usual way. He made sure I came before he did. After his orgasm, he kept kissing and caressing me and before I realized what he was doing, he was going down on me. I had an orgasm and another. He continued pleasuring me orally and manually until I was exhausted. I learned something that night. He loved doing it. Men love giving us pleasure. They feel so powerful when they can be good lovers to us. Why are we so hung up on being pleasured?"

Other women report they began to have orgasms during intercourse or multiple orgasms during lovemaking when they gave themselves permission to touch their own clitorises. Sometimes you need that extra touch. Rather than hoping he'll touch you—or hoping you'll get sufficient indirect stimulation—touch yourself.

Use the Mental Preparation Techniques of Easily Orgasmic Women. (See page 9 for descriptions of starting on warm; indulging in erotic entertainment; conveying intentions; mental preimaging.)

"I can have multiple orgasms when I lay the groundwork for them," Carla said. "It's most likely to happen when I've taken time to prepare for lovemaking with the bubble bath, the glass of wine, the fantasies. My husband knows to leave me alone in the tub when

I take my glass of wine to the bathroom. That's my time for getting all worked up in my head."

Now that you are in the right mental state for multiple orgasms, you need only a few physical tricks for making them happen.

*T*ECHNIQUES FOR ACHIEVING MULTIPLES

Alternating Stimuli

During lovemaking, alternate physical stimuli to achieve multiple orgasms. The first one or two orgasms, for example, may be via oral or manual stimulation. Women who do have multiples report they seldom have them during lovemaking sessions that began with intercourse.

Her partner will increase the odds by giving her the *first orgasm via cunnilingus.* Oral sex more fully arouses the female genitalia, making orgasm during intercourse more likely. He should continue stimulating her after she has reached orgasm by manually stroking her rather than immediately entering her. If she experiences a second orgasm either orally or manually, she may find that intercourse seems to spread the sensations throughout her body. Many women report that the heightened sensitivity they feel after an orgasm or two via cunnilingus and/or manual stimulation makes intercourse a more sensual experience.

"An oral orgasm seems to open the door to more orgasms for me in a way that a first orgasm by any other means doesn't," Lisa explained. "Oral orgasms generate wider concentric waves of pleasure throughout my lower body. Other orgasms can be more intense, but they don't start out as wide.

"When I have intercourse after an oral orgasm or two, the thrusting doesn't seem localized in the vagina. It's as if his penis is stirring sensations throughout my body via my vagina."

And Shelley, who *only* has multiple orgasms if the first one is via cunnilingus, said, "Orgasms come faster and easier for me through cunnilingus than any other way. Once I have the first one, the others come easier. If I am only receiving manual stimulation or indirect stimulation from intercourse, I will have an orgasm, but it takes longer. I'm not set up at that point for multiples. They just won't happen."

Continued and varied genital stimulation after cunnilingus keeps the woman's level of arousal high. Think of her orgasmic pattern as a graph line with peaks and valleys. If the stimulation stops after an orgasm, her arousal state drops. She has further to climb to reach the next peak. Maintaining varied stimulation keeps the level of arousal high without painful sensitivity.

Manual Contact

Touching is critical in the quest for multiple orgasms. Women who aren't comfortable touching themselves during sex are far less likely to experience multiples—because they have to depend on their partners to know exactly when and how to apply the stimulation that would take them from one peak to the next. Even the best lovers can't always get that right.

By stroking herself during cunnilingus or intercourse, a woman can be sure she gets the variety of stimulation she needs. Many women have longer, more intense orgasms during masturbation by varying the stimulus to the clitoral area. When they feel orgasm approaching, they move the stimulus away from the area surrounding the clitoris, perhaps massaging the outer vaginal lips or thrusting their fingers deeper inside the vagina. They return to the clitoral area when the urge to reach orgasm ebbs somewhat but not significantly.

"I use the same masturbatory techniques I use alone in addition to my partner's lovemaking to increase the number or duration of the orgasmic spasms," said Cathy. "I rarely have multiples if I don't touch myself. I know when, where, and how. It's a magic spot and a magic moment. A partner might hit it right once in ten tries. I know I always will."

And Angie said, "I can begin to come again—for the second or third or fourth time—almost as soon as my husband enters me, if he uses slow, shallow strokes for a while and manipulates the area surrounding my clitoris with his finger or thumb. That triggers my clitoris to send me off into another orgasm. Once I start coming again, he thrusts deeper and faster, making the orgasm last and, if I'm lucky, spill right into another one."

Repeated Direct Stimuli

Some women report that they are most likely to experience multiple orgasms not when the stimuli is varied, but when their partners repeatedly stimulate the clitoral area in the same way. (There are exceptions to every rule.) A few women need constant, concerted stimulation at the same focal point to have multiple orgasms.

"If my partner can keep his tongue in the same place, I can come over and over again," Mary said. "If he moves, I lose the momentum."

Michel, the gigolo, claims that the best technique a man can use to supply repeated stimuli is:

- THE FLAME. Pretend the tip of your tongue is a candle flame. In your mind's eye, see that flame flickering in the wind. Move your tongue rapidly around the sides of her clitoris, above and below it, as the candle flame moves.

  "Some women only have multiples during cunnilingus when I continue to lick the sides of the clitoris in slow, even strokes," he said. "If I hit it just right, these women can have intense multiple orgasms—so intense one woman almost passed out."

G Spot Multiples

Some women only have multiples when they are receiving both clitoral and vaginal stimulation in the area of the G spot. To make this happen, a man should use his fingers to stimulate the front wall of her vagina while he's performing cunnilingus. Or, during intercourse, he or she should stimulate the clitoris.

"I need the total sensation to have multiples," said Karen. "I can have an orgasm via clitoral or G spot stimulation, but I won't have multiples unless both areas are being stroked and massaged."

She added, "I have them most often when we follow cunnilingus with manual stimulation followed by intercourse in the rear-entry position with him stroking my clit. I think in rear-entry position, I get more direct G spot stimulation."

Finally, some women cannot predict what will cause them to have multiple orgasms. It may be her mood or the quality of her fantasies before sex or her partner or even her hormone balance. And some women who are capable of having multiples say they do not have them unless they are with a partner they trust completely.

Can they tell when lovemaking will lead to multiple orgasms?

"When I'm going to have multiples, I feel my body throbbing," said Michele. "The pulse pounds in my clitoris. I know it's going to happen. But I don't know that until I'm pretty far along into the experience."

Other women report similar feelings, which they may describe as throbbing or pulsating. Or they say their whole bodies become taut and their clitorises feel like little stone monuments. I know I'm going to have multiples when the first orgasm doesn't feel like a complete release, when I've become aroused to the point where it will take several orgasms to release the tension.

Are many ever too many? Not for the majority, but for some women they can be.

"Yes, sometimes one can be enough," said Gail. "Depending on how long my lover has stimulated my clitoris, the orgasms can become almost painful, too intense. Most of the time, I prefer one big orgasm, then a lot of space, say fifteen minutes or so, before another one. Too close together leaves me ready to jump out of my skin at the next touch."

And another woman said, "I am not always open to the intensity of having multiple orgasms. It leaves me feeling vulnerable somehow. I don't always like the feeling."

MALE MULTIPLES

The man who brought the concept of multiple male orgasms to the mainstream self-help movement is Stan Dale, who has a doctorate in Human Sexuality from the Institute for the Advanced Study of Sexuality in San Francisco. He said he discovered the difference between ejaculation and orgasm when he was required to ejaculate into a small jar for the obligatory sperm count test a month after his vasectomy. After fifteen minutes of the "most unsensuous masturbation" of his life, Dale finally produced the required sample. As he was walking back to the nurse's desk, he thought to himself, "That was a nonorgasmic ejaculation."

Nonorgasmic ejaculation?

"Yes, I had experienced a cold-blooded, clinical, *physical* ejaculation without an orgasm. Alarmed, I called my doctor. She laughed and said, 'Congratulations! You've found out the difference between ejaculation and orgasm. Now enjoy yourself.'"

Thus began his quest for the orgasm without ejaculation— which led to his personal discovery of male multiple orgasms. How did he achieve this feat? By using his mind to control the ejaculatory process. And how is this different than reciting baseball statistics to prolong intercourse?

"When I felt the oncoming urge to ejaculate, I told myself, consciously at first, 'Not yet, hold off, later maybe.' This didn't always work, and when it did, it involved a deliberate mental effort. But practice makes perfect. Little by little, my involuntary sexual reactions began to respond more and more automatically to the directions from my mind. I was thinking less and feeling more until that glorious occasion when, with no conscious effort, pure feeling took over and I experienced for the first time the unimaginable ecstasy of unbidden total orgasm. Without ejaculation!"

In a few men orgasm without ejaculation is the result of retrograde ejaculation, which occurs when the semen is forced back into the bladder rather than out the urethra due to a malfunction in the valve between the urethra and bladder. This sometimes occurs in men who have had prostate or bladder surgery. It is not painful—and does not affect the quality of the orgasm.

Through the Human Awareness Institute, which he founded, Dale has been facilitating "Sex, Love, and Intimacy" workshops for twenty-five years in northern California, Chicago, and countries as far away as Japan and Australia, where he preaches the credo of multiple orgasms for men. A former radio announcer who was the voice of *The Shadow* and the narrator of *The Lone Ranger,* Dale is handsome and charismatic. But his workshops are long on New Age spiritual psychobabble and short on technique.

A man who took one of his men-only workshops taped the lecture on male multiple orgasms with Dale's permission.

"Welcome to the room of love," he greeted workshop participants in a rich baritone.

Nice voice, but the technique part of the talk consisted of three incomplete steps.

- Learn to control the sphincter muscle by holding back your stool when you defecate and then letting it out.

- To strengthen the PC muscles, start to urinate, then stop; repeat several times. Practice frequently.

- When about to ejaculate, attempt to hold it back. This may cause some pain at first, but soon you will be able to delay ejaculation for amazingly long periods of time.

Why these few sketchy directions? (You'd think he could at least provide full instructions for performing kegels for the $625 workshop fee.)

"There are no rules for jumping into the new because no one has ever been there before!" Dale told me.

Clearly the man has not studied the teachings of the ancient sexologists.

THE TECHNIQUES

Repeated Use of the Three-Finger Method or the Big Draw

- Use the Taoist techniques—the three-finger method or the big draw on pages 185–186—more than once during lovemaking.

  One man said, "I have not only prolonged lovekmaking, but have also experienced orgasm without ejaculation— sometimes several times during a lovemaking session—by repeating the three-finger method when I am close to ejaculation, up to three or four times. The next day my balls feel a little tender, but it's worth it."

Men who have experienced orgasm without ejaculation say that it feels like orgasm *with* ejaculation, sometimes more diffuse. Some note that they didn't realize they were having a nonejaculatory orgasm at first because the feeling was so similar. When they did not lose their erections following orgasm, they knew something different had happened to them.

"I have the contractions," one man said, "the same as I do when I ejaculate. But the contractions seem less localized in the penis. I feel them reverberating more throughout the genital area, even in the tops of my thighs and my lower belly."

And some men who are adept at delaying ejaculation say that they began having multiple orgasms as a result of the delaying techniques.

"I wasn't trying to have multiple orgasms," a man told me. "I just found myself having them as a result of prolonging intercourse by using the big draw. First, I realized I was having an orgasm without ejaculating. And I was still very hard after the orgasm."

The Art of Brinkmanship

Some men train themselves to experience orgasm without ejaculation fairly easily using the art of brinkmanship: pulling back at the last possible second before ejaculation.

- Practice while masturbating, when you can focus entirely on your own process of arousal.

- Continue stimulation to the point of impending orgasm. Then stop.

- Do not resume stimulation until your arousal level has declined.

- Repeat as often as possible. With practice, you should be able to experience the contractions of orgasmic release without ejaculating.

"I have been able to enjoy penetration up to a half an hour before having the first of a series of multiple orgasms without ejaculation," said Mark. "I began teaching myself to pull back on the brink of orgasm just to make intercourse last longer. When I was close to orgasm, I would withdraw and stimulate my wife with my hand, then reinsert my penis when I was less aroused. I found I could manipulate my arousal level that way, bringing myself higher and higher each time before I pulled out. One night after I had backed off repeatedly from ejaculating, I found myself having an orgasm without ejaculating. It was an extraordinary and intense experience. I came several times that night before I finally ejaculated, which was more powerful than anything I'd ever felt in my life."

The Valley, a Multiple-Orgasm Technique for Men

Mantak Chia calls orgasm with ejaculation "the Peak Orgasm—one fleeting moment of intense, even excruciating pleasure, then nothing." The Valley Orgasm is "a continual rolling expansion of the orgasm, a greatly heightened ecstasy"—like a series of orgasms, without ejaculation.

- First, make love using the "nine shallow, one deep" method of thrusting (see page 170).

- Stop thrusting when you feel near orgasm.

- Use the big draw (see page 186) to delay ejaculation.

- Hold your partner in a close, comfortable embrace. Continue shallow thrusting.

- Each time you feel ejaculation is imminent, use the big draw. You will experience the sensations of orgasm, though more diffuse, without ejaculation.

Mark said, "Combining the coital dynamics with the big draw does produce the series of orgasms. You bring yourself close, then pull back with the big draw, then increase the stimulation through coital dynamics again, and so forth. But you really have to practice to make this happen. Your PCs have to be in shape. I found other methods easier."

The Perineum Halt—How She Can Help

You can either induce or delay male orgasm by manipulating the perineum. Yes, this is confusing. Whether you induce or delay depends in part of the man's responsiveness to the maneuver and in part on when and with how much pressure it is performed and whether you use the thumb or three fingers. Review the techniques and practice (see pages 184 and 204). Some of the men who have tested these methods for me claim pressure on the perineum stops them from ejaculating, while others swear it induces orgasm. This is not an exact science.

You can also stop his orgasm—sometimes—by placing the tip of your index finger against his anus, pressing the rest of the finger tightly against his skin as you cup his balls with your hand, pulling them away from his body. This takes practice and cooperation. Don't perform it on an unwilling partner.

A woman said, "My boyfriend and I have been able to delay his orgasms sometimes using this. He says, 'Stop me,' and I use the maneuver while he pulls his penis almost all the way out of my vagina. If we do this several times during lovemaking, we can bring on multiple orgasms for him. The added bonus is that he gets to the point where he is dying to ejaculate after having orgasms without ejaculating—and he makes love like a wild man."

Part 7

TAKING IT TO THE LIMIT

Chapter Fifteen

EXTENDED AND WHOLE-BODY ORGASMS

*W*e didn't think we could do this at first," Danielle said. "But we have learned to go beyond making our orgasms last longer. We have taken orgasm to a higher dimension. The erotic arousal begins in the genitals and spreads throughout our bodies. When we begin to orgasm, we experience it as a flooding of ecstasy throughout the body, not like regular orgasms, which are little waves that crash against the genitals and quickly dissipate.

"We got this seminar for a wedding present from a friend in London," explained Danielle, a petite, dark, and ebullient French artist in her mid-thirties recently married to Piet, a Dutch business-man in his late twenties. The couple lives in Amsterdam, where Piet was born. "We would never have thought of this for ourselves, though we both do a little yoga as part of our fitness routines.

"The people who are deeply involved in this are cultists," she said. "Piet and I have lives outside the bedroom. 'What is in this for us?' we asked at first.

"Sexual ecstasy is a higher form of lovemaking and it's very re-warding. Just as you won't have a gourmet meal every night of the week, you won't always make love this way. When you do, it is an emotional experience in which orgasm time is expanded, in our case up to ten or fifteen minutes. Some of the couples say they are having even longer orgasms.

"People do get bored with sex if it doesn't change. For us, this is another way of ensuring we will not become bored with each other."

Sexual ecstasy, or high sex as it is known in some Tantric circles, is a way of making love that expands arousal and orgasm beyond the genitals and extends the time period of orgasmic response—giving lovers both extended and whole-body orgasms. Serious practitioners *are* cultists. Few people can find accessible seminars where they can learn the basic techniques and then modify them to suit their lifestyles. Most training in high sex is offered by gurus who limit attendance in their programs to those couples who are already proficient in Tantra and whose lives revolve around the practice. ("Are you one with The Source?" a prominent California guru asked me. "If you are not, I cannot share this secret and magic technique for achieving the ultimate sexual union of seven chakra sex.")

Unlike the dogmatists—many of whom have received significantly less training than she has—Margo Anand, who conducts sexual ecstasy seminars in Europe and California, is more receptive to the uninitiated. (However, she primarily teaches The Love and Ecstasy Training, three ten-day seminars held over a one-year period. Participants are expected to work on the training between sessions.) An attractive dark-haired woman who appears to be around forty, Anand has a master's degree in psychology and philosophy from the Sorbonne and thousands of hours of instruction in bodywork therapies, bioenergetics, encounter, rolfing, Gestalt, and other esoteric disciplines. She studied yoga with the renowned Swami Satchitananda. In the seventies she joined the faculty of the Arica institute in New York, founded by South American mystic Oscar Ichazo. The institute blended martial arts, Sufism, the teachings of Gurdjieff, and other spiritual traditions. At approximately the same time, she discovered Tantra.

"Unlike most mystical paths, Tantra included sexuality as a

doorway to ecstasy and enlightenment," she said. "I was immediately intrigued."

Tantra was established five thousand years ago in India as a rebellion against the Brahmins, the Hindu priesthood, who preached sexual denial in the pursuit of spiritual enlightenment. The Tantrics worshiped the god Shiva and his consort, the goddess Shakti, who they believed united the spiritual and the sexual. The Tantric tradition was carried to Tibet around the tenth century. Scattered underground cults were said to exist as far away as Athens and may have influenced some of the erotic traditions for prolonging pleasure and extending orgasm that exist in many cultures around the world, including Chinese, Native American, Polynesian, Egyptian, Scandinavian, and African.

However they came into being, those traditions include a variety of techniques unknown in Western culture. One ancient Polynesian sexual practice, for example, recommends an hour-long embrace of intercourse during which man and woman alternate periods of gentle movement with stillness to encourage a long and gentle orgasm. The ancient Arabs practiced Imsak, the arabic word for "retention," in which the man pulled out when he felt close to ejaculating and continued to stimulate the woman with his hand or mouth, until he was able to resume thrusting again. He would do this repeatedly, up to ten times per night, both to prolong her pleasure by multiplying and extending her orgasms and his own by delaying climax.

In America, however, most men learned in adolescence how to ejaculate as quickly as possible to avoid being caught masturbating—and most women learned that an orgasm wasn't nearly as "important" as the feelings of closeness generated by lovemaking. There has been enough sex guilt to go around the table several times in this country, ensuring that each one of us, male and female, was dished an ample helping. No surprise that American sex today is goal-oriented: get to intercourse, orgasm, and good night.

For us, the idea of making bliss last beyond the few seconds Masters and Johnson told us we could have seems as likely as the existence of flying saucers. But what if those sexperts in the white lab coats were underestimating our potential? Suspend disbelief for the moment and beam on up.

*T*HE PATH TO SEXUAL ECSTASY—EXTENDED AND WHOLE-BODY

Eight couples seated in a lecture room at the New Ancient Sex Academy in Amsterdam nodded in agreement as Margo Anand, the seminar leader, asked, "Haven't you ever wondered, 'Isn't there more to sex than this?'

"Haven't you ever felt incomplete during sex because your partner has already landed before you have had a chance to take off?

"Have you ever felt bored with sex in a long-term relationship and found yourself wishing you could recapture the passion that used to make sex between you so exciting?

"Have you ever glimpsed an ecstatic moment in love and later felt that you don't know the way back?"

With these questions, Anand put sexual ecstasy in a familiar perspective. Most of us don't want to pursue a sexual/spiritual training that will teach us to *replace* the explosions of genital sex with the more subtle and diffuse whole-body response she defined as "the timeless joy of ecstasy." Frankly, most of us will never have, or take, the time to spend hours in a genital embrace. What about the laundry, the gym, the kids' soccer practice, dinner with friends? Yes, we want more pleasure, but we don't want to give up explosive orgasms to get deeper, longer, stronger orgasms. We want it all. And if our orgasms can spread from a genital explosion throughout our whole bodies—great. Can we do this in the thirty minutes or less left over for lovemaking tonight?

By adapting the teachings of Tantra to the realities of your modern life, you probably can, at least sometimes. First, practice lengthening and stretching your orgasm while masturbating.

Stretching Orgasm Exercise, His

• Masturbate without ejaculating for as long as you can. (The goal in this exercise is thirty minutes. The reality is often ten to fifteen minutes.) Do this by stopping and/or changing strokes when ejaculation is imminent.

• Count the contractions you feel upon ejaculation, normally between three and eight. Note the level and order of intensity. Typically the strongest contractions will be at the beginning.

• The next time you masturbate, again delay ejaculation as long as possible.

• When you do ejaculate, flex the PC muscles as you would to retard ejaculation. Then continue stimulating your penis very slowly while squeezing throughout the ejaculation—pushing the sensations on and on.

The men who tried this reported they doubled their orgasm time after a few practice sessions. One man said, "I was surprised at how easy it is to increase orgasm time this way. The orgasm feels a little different, less intense at the beginning, more intense than it would normally be at the end."

Spreading Orgasm Exercise, Hers

• Masturbate in a comfortable position, possibly using the strokes described on page 65.

• As soon as you become highly aroused, use the other hand to massage with light, shallow strokes the area of the vulva, inner thighs, and groin. Imagine that you are spreading the arousal throughout those areas. Continue the massage throughout your orgasm, imagining you are spreading the orgasm into your body.

• After orgasm, continue rhythmic stroking in the genital area. (Some women find the clitoris too sensitive immediately after orgasm for further stimulation.) Feel the orgasm continuing to spread throughout your body several seconds after it would have normally dissipated.

The women who tried this also reported success. One said, "The orgasm does seem to spread throughout the body as you massage and fantasize about it doing so. But I found the experience more satisfying when my partner massaged while I masturbated."

EXTENDED ORGASMS

Now that you have discovered how relatively easy it is to expand your orgasm during masturbation, you're ready to extend the experience to lovemaking. You can teach your partner to pleasure you incorporating the same techniques you used during masturbation. And you can move on to other love games designed to extend orgasms.

Staying on the Edge

• Begin by taking a cool, not hot, shower together so that your skin will be cool to each other's touch and you'll feel relaxed. Lie on the bed in the X, or scissors, position (see page 162). The man does not need to have an erection. In fact, it's better if he doesn't because it will take him that much longer to ejaculate.

• Insert his flaccid penis into the vagina, which will contract around the penis as long as both remain still. You may have to keep your hand around the base of his penis to hold him in place for a few minutes until the vagina does contract and/or he has a moderate erection.

• Breathing deeply, remain motionless for thirty minutes. During that time, caress each other's faces, necks, and upper bodies and make frequent, prolonged eye contact. This is a good time for whispered terms of endearment.

• Begin moving together. He should be thrusting slowly and gently and she should be matching his pace with her pelvis and hips. Kiss deeply. As you move your bodies, use your hands to stroke each other, working upward from the genitals. Imagine you are spreading fire with your hands.

• Resist the desire to move faster when you reach that agonizing point of being "almost there." You want to stay on the verge for as long as possible—until you realize you are having an orgasm, which will seem to last forever.

If you put the time into this, you can have a unique orgasmic experience. My partner and I found that resisting the temptation to get into a different position and just *do it* was impossible the first time we tried. The next day we practiced greater control and really did reach the point where it was impossible to tell when the orgasm had begun or how long it had lasted. Exhausting, yet exhilarating. My panel of testers rated this a "special" way of lovemaking, something they would reserve for those nights when they want to pamper each other or, as one woman said, "reconnect after a frenzied week." Another woman said, "This is not for the nights when you are desperately hungry for each other. You need the slow beginning to get to the place where it feels like your body is riding on molten waves and you can't tell the difference between arousal and orgasm." And her partner said, "We dubbed it 'the slowie,' the polar opposite of the quickie."

Karezza

Karezza, an Italian word that means "caress," is the name given to a technique developed in 1883 by an American physician, Alice Bunker Stockham. She borrowed it in part from a pamphlet on birth control written by a founding member of the Oneida community, a minister who adapted it in part from ancient erotic teachings. Stockham instructed her married patients in the art of karezza as a way to prevent premature ejaculation while allowing sufficient time for female arousal. Her small self-published book, *Karezza: Ethics of Marriage,* was translated into several languages, including Russian by the great novelist Leo Tolstoy.

As a technique for prolonging intercourse, it is simple and effective and can be practiced in any position. It also encourages extended orgasm, if you ignore the more esoteric parts of Stockham's advice. She told her patients to prepare for karezza by reading uplifting writings, such as those of Ralph Waldo Emerson and Elizabeth Barrett Browning. She also thought that lovers should remain in the position for an hour of quiet sexual union, possibly discussing the meaning of the writings they'd just read. Neither the man nor the woman was supposed to reach orgasm during this tranquil period.

Thousands of years before Stockham named karezza, the great Chinese physician Master Sun taught a similar technique to men as a way of giving their women great pleasure. The men were not allowed to have an orgasm, the women were encouraged to have many.

In our time, Xavier Hollander was an advocate of karezza as a means of extending female orgasm.

Karezza for Modern Lovers

- Drastically limit his genital movement. The man does not move inside the women unless he becomes flaccid—and only then is he to use sufficient shallow thrusts to revive his erection. The missionary position is probably the one least likely to encourage karezza. Female superior or side by side are better choices.

• She is allowed movement, including thrusting her hips against his or contracting her PC muscles around his penis. No matter how excited she gets, he takes only sufficient thrusting strokes to maintain an erection.

• Using the masturbatory technique of spreading, the woman or her partner encourages the spread of her orgasm throughout her body.

• The man holds their lovemaking embrace until his partner has achieved one or several orgasms. Then he is free to move with more energy and satisfy himself if he so desires.

A self-described "former premature ejaculator" who has had great success with this method claimed he can make intercourse last thirty minutes—or longer than most of his partners have needed to reach one or more orgasms. "Nothing else has enabled me to last so long," he said. Another man, who studied with karezza master J. William Lloyd, said, "Ejaculation is no longer the whole point. My wife has learned to have extended orgasms during karezza. I can continue to the point where I no longer want to ejaculate but am thoroughly fulfilled in having satisfied her." And a woman said, "This is nice for a change of pace. I do find an orgasm seems to last longer using this method. But I don't have the big explosive orgasms I like best. It depends on what mood you are in. My husband and I are glad we've learned new ways of making love."

The Nine-Course Meal—The Extended Orgasm for Women Only

A male colleague who is a leading sex therapist attended a seminar in San Francisco several years ago conducted by Dr. Stephen Chang, one of the world's foremost authorities on ancient Taoist medical practices. This seminar was based on *Su Nui Ching,* or *The White Madame's Classic,* a work attributed to the Emperor Huang Ti, who ruled China from 2697 to 2597 B.C. This classic work of sexology disappeared in China over a thousand years ago and has been only recently rediscovered.

According to the *Su Nui Ching,* Dr. Chang said, the woman should be served a nine-course erotic meal by her man.

"I liked the idea," my friend said, "and put it to use in my own marriage. But I thought it too one-sided to use in my practice."

"The woman's role in this form of loveplay is to let go completely, while the man's role is to fulfill her, to serve her."

The nine courses are marked by physical signs. The attentive Tao lover notes the sign that she has reached one stage and then adapts his lovemaking to bring her to the next. He begins by kissing. As her excitement level increases, he moves down her body, making love to her breasts, back to her mouth, down her body to her genitals. Through a combination of cunnilingus and manual clitoral stimulation, he brings her to a deep orgasm, which he spreads through her body by massaging her with his free hand or hands.

According to the book, the signs, or steps, are:

1. *She sighs and her breath grows short.*
2. *Her heartbeat accelerates.*
3. *Her saliva increases.*
4. *Her vaginal secretions grow thicker.*
5. *She holds him ferociously in her embrace.*
6. *She starts to bite or nibble.*
7. *She perspires heavily.*
8. *Her skin feels softer, and her muscles begin to go slack.*
9. *She has a total orgasm.*

A man said, "My wife was never bitten me. She's not a biter. I don't think every woman will show every sign. By looking for the signs, a man becomes exquisitely sensitive to the changes in his partner's arousal level, noticing things he never noticed before. He is so keenly aware of her that he makes the right moves and can bring her to a climax so deep and intense and long-lasting he almost feels it himself. Indeed, I typically do have an orgasm as she is coming down from hers, even though I didn't realize I was anywhere near the ejaculation point." And another man who tried this said, "By devoting myself totally to my wife's pleasure and paying closer attention to her responses than I ever had, I learned a great deal about how she does respond to my lovemaking. I should have done this years ago. I lost myself in making love to her for the first time in our three years together."

Kabbazah—The Extended Orgasm for Men Only

"I first experienced kabbazah in Japan when I was on R&R leave from Vietnam," said Michael, who served two tours of duty as a fighter pilot in the war. "The Japanese prostitute told me she would give me the sexual experience of my life if I was willing to pay triple the going rate. We negotiated. Her going rate was already higher than average, but she was beautiful and I was horny. I told her I would pay half in advance and half later if it really was the sexual experience of my life. She insisted on two-thirds up front, one third later. I didn't have anything else to do with my money, so I said, 'Give it to me, babe.'

"She took my cock in her hands and it sprang to life. Then she told me to lie back and not move. She was adamant on this point. 'I do man's work,' she said. She climbed on top of me. Not moving was hard at first. I was horny as hell. And she barely moved her body herself. What she moved was the muscles inside her vagina. She fucked me with those muscles, good and slow. The sensations were incredible, unlike anything I'd ever felt inside a woman. She brought me to a long, slow orgasm that lasted so long.

"I gave her six times her going rate. It was that good. And for years I searched unsuccessfully for a woman who could do what she did for me."

Michael's story has a happy ending. Recently, his wife read about kabbazah in an Eastern sex book and learned to perform it.

Thousands of years ago in the Middle East, at a time when that part of the world was not dominated by religious extremists, a woman who had mastered the art of *pompoir* (control of the PC muscles during intercourse, see page 174) was called a *kabbazah,* or "one who holds." *Kabbazahs* included the best prostitutes in many Eastern countries, including China, Japan, and India. Prostitution was sacred in India and the temple prostitutes believed that they brought a man to religious as well as sexual ecstasy via kabbazah. The lifestyle of these Eastern prostitutes was the equivalent of that enjoyed by today's most expensive call girls, like the women brought from the United States and Europe to service the sexual needs of rich Arabs at their lavish parties.

In her own way, Michael's Japanese prostitute carried on the sacred sex tradition of the Indian temple prostitutes, who were trained in the technique from childhood. Even today, in some parts of Africa, young women receive kabbazah training. And most women who consult sex therapists are told to practice their kegels to improve sex. In researching this book, I was struck by how sexologists and sex therapists of the late twentieth century have developed theories and techniques that are similar to the theories and techniques espoused and practiced by the sex experts of thousands of years ago. A really good idea never dies.

The kabbazah can be a wonderful treat for a man when he's in a passive mood, perhaps too tired to get the sexual pleasure he desires. Increasingly, men are willing to admit they enjoy playing the passive role sometimes. What's in this for the woman? The excitement of being in charge, of being in control of a sexual situation in which the man remains absolutely passive. And the pleasure of giving.

The requirements for this technique are twofold:

- He must be in a relaxed and receptive state of mind and body. His passivity is crucial. Again, this is not the kind of sex you have when you are desperately tearing each other's clothing off the minute the door closes behind you.

- She must have a virtuoso vagina. The woman should have achieved mastery of the PC muscles through diligent practice of kegels for at least a period of three weeks to a month.

Some couples find that a period of abstinence, two or three days to a week, intensifies the experience, while others report that abstinence makes it impossible for the man to remain passive. Some positions are better than others. Try female superior or one of the sitting positions.

- She stimulates her partner until he is just erect, not highly aroused, and inserts his penis.

- He does not move his pelvis at all. Never. Not once.

- She also strives for no pelvic movement, confining all movement, or as much as possible, to her PC muscles.

- You may caress or kiss each other.

- She flexes her muscles in varying patterns until she feels his penis throbbing, which should occur approximately fifteen minutes into kabbazah and indicates an intense level of arousal.

- She times her contractions to the throbbing of his penis, clenching and releasing in time with him.

- In another ten to fifteen minutes, he will experience a longer, more intense orgasm than normal. He may or may not ejaculate.

A woman said, "I feel like a goddess when I give my lover kabbazah. Afterward I lie in his arms while he strokes me to orgasm with his hand. It's a long, strong orgasm."

Another woman reported, "At the end of kabbazah, I flex my PC muscles like mad and have a tremendous orgasm. It is like ending a summer picnic with a fireworks display."

WHOLE-BODY ORGASMS

"Sometimes I feel the tremors all over my body during orgasm," said Jane. "First my body gets taut. It's like my breasts and nipples and vaginal walls are expanding. They feel bigger and bigger. My whole body is alive and aroused and quivering. The orgasms start in my genitals, like waves in my clitoris, my outer lips, my vagina, deep inside the walls. The waves grow bigger and spread throughout my body until I can even feel them in the tips of my fingers and my toes.

"I see colors flashing, bright primary colors. It's a transcendent experience that lifts me outside of my body and puts me back down again."

Other people who have experienced them describe whole-body orgasms in similar ways. "The orgasm blew out the top of my head and spewed out my toes," a woman said. And a man called his first whole-body orgasm "almost an out-of-body experience because it was so intense it seemed to take me out of my body and put me back again." Some describe the event as being swept away by a tidal wave or rocked by an earthquake. One woman said, "The earth really did move this time."

It is possible to have intense orgasms and multiple orgasms and extended orgasms without experiencing a whole-body orgasm. And some only have whole-body orgasms during masturbation.

"After a period of continuous penis massage, using various combinations of strokes, I clench all my muscles from head to toe, hold the breath for half a minute, and then release it," said Michael. "The combined flooding of breath and erotic energies can trigger a full-body orgasm with profound effects."

Some people experience whole-body orgasms only when they

have a strong emotional connection to their partners. Others when they are feeling particularly sensual or sexual or both. The WBO is most likely the result of intense connection on three levels—emotional, sensual, and sexual—though again, this is not true for everyone.

Consider the levels to be separate doors, three possible ways into the whole body orgasm.

Emotional

Master Meugi of Singapore teaches Kundaliani yoga, a form of sexual yoga, mostly to wealthy women from all over the world who are living in Singapore because their husbands have jobs or diplomatic assignments there. These women pass his name around in their select circles the way they exchange information about hairdressers, manicurists, or personal trainers. I met Meugi in Bombay when he stopped en route to the Third Asian Conference of Sexuality.

"Can you have a whole-body orgasm through Kundaliani?" I asked him.

"Whole-body orgasms can be simple," he said. And then he described intricate positions that are conducive to the experience, positions that can be obtained only after years of serious devotion to yoga.

I had trouble imagining bevies of international wives, with their myriad family and social responsibilities, twisted into any of these poses, much less having orgasms while there. When I pressed Meugi further, he conceded that a whole-body orgasm was indeed possible in a relatively simple position, the yabyum (see page 184), and when the man and woman practice the Tantric yoga kiss.

Like the eye lock (see page 183), the kiss encourages an emotional as well as physical closeness between the partners. According to Tantric belief, the soul of one flows into the soul of another during the kiss, and the energy of one becomes the energy of the other. Souls aside, the intimacy of the Tantric kiss can intensify the orgasm for both and certainly can lead to a whole-body orgasm—if they are in the mood for that kind of loving.

- *THE TANTRIC YOGA KISS.* The man should use one of the methods on pages 185–187 to delay his orgasm and ejaculation during lovemaking. When the woman feels her orgasm is imminent, she should signal to the man. They stop making love in whatever position they are in. They sit in the middle of the bed with their legs wrapped around each other in the yabyum position, his penis inside her, and remain as still as possible. Pressing their foreheads together, they breathe into each other's mouths. As he exhales she inhales and vice versa. Prolong the "kiss" for at least ten minutes, if possible. At some point, remaining still will no longer be an option. Any movement at all will hopefully trigger orgasm.

One of my testers said, "This worked for my husband and me. We both had orgasms that felt like they could blow the tops of our heads off." Another couple reported, "We didn't have what either of us considered a full-body orgasm, but we did have stronger orgasms. He said he felt his orgasm throughout his genitals in a much deeper way than usual, even inside his bowels. And my orgasm was stronger, definitely confined to the clitoris, vagina, and anus, with one exception: It radiated down inside my thighs all the way to the backs of my knees."

Sensual and Sexual

Strange de Jim, a self-described "masseur extraordinaire" from the Caribbean, claims he "invented metasexual lovemaking," which is really another version of the whole-body orgasm.

Strange is a difficult man to track down. He may promise to give a class or seminar and then not show up—as he did at the New Ancient Sex Academy in Amsterdam, where I had planned to hear him speak. On the other hand, he may casually drop by a workshop taught by another instructor and give an impromptu demonstration of massage techniques. I met him quite by accident at the Sex Museum (also in Amsterdam), where he was explaining metasexual massage to a group of Norwegian tourists who seemed to be captivated and alarmed by him in equal measure.

"You have to take a professional massage course and give one hundred free one-hour massages before you can begin to understand the sensitivity, energy, and state of mind that lead to extraordinary lovemaking," he said. "True sex is awakening that quiet exquisite being on the inside. The orgasm comes from the inside."

Later, when I challenged him to provide a shortcut—some useful advice for the sexual adventurer who doesn't have one hundred hours to commit to giving massages—he admitted that a book on erotic massage techniques, a little masturbatory practice, and the mastery of "three games" could bring you to something approaching his idea of extraordinary sex.

The first "game" is an expansion of the big draw method for delaying ejaculation.

"The other two games are based on the active partner being extremely focused and the passive partner being completely relaxed and receptive," he said. "In the first game the active partner turns on the passive partner so much that he or she is brought to orgasm through extragenital touch"—that is, by touching any part of the body except the genitals.

- *THE BIGGER DRAW.* Follow the basic instructions for the big draw (see page 186), but add a lot more muscle. Pull back to approximately one inch of penetration, but do not entirely withdraw. Flex not only the PC muscles but every muscle, from head to toe, and hold for half a minute as you are simultaneously holding your breath. Release muscles and breath. The combined flooding of breath and relaxing of muscles can trigger a whole-body orgasm.

A man who tried this successfully said, "I think holding the breath is the key part. It has the same effect as hyperventilating. It takes you to a different place." And another man said, "This worked for me after a long lovemaking session in which I had repeatedly held myself back from ejaculating. It is definitely worth the wait and effort, a truly mind-blowing experience, which brought tears to my eyes."

• *THE EXTRAGENITAL ORGASM.* Caress your partner's genitals orally and manually (see techniques previously detailed on pages 103–104) until he (or she) is on the verge of orgasm, then shift attention to nongenital areas. Alternate from genital stimulation to nongenital, until he is so aroused—in a state of hypersensitivity—that you can bring him to orgasm by, for example, running a finger down his inner thigh. The orgasm will feel like it begins in the genitals and expands throughout the whole body.

My partner and I tried this on each other. He was able to bring me to orgasm by sucking my nipples and, on a second occasion, by licking my inner thigh. They were intense orgasms, but no more "whole body" than other orgasms I've experienced after intense stimulation. He was not able to reach orgasm through extragenital stimulation, got frustrated with the game, and begged for fellatio. Other couples testing the method did report success. One woman said, "I was able to have a whole-body orgasm from having my breasts sucked. The orgasms started in my nipples and spread out like concentric radiant circles over every inch of me inside and out." Her partner? "No such luck."

Strange de Jim's second game requires an adept tongue and knowledge of the exact location of your partner's perineum, the point between anus and genitals in both sexes, also called the "prostate point" in the male. And, as previously noted, manipulating the perineum has different results in different people, and sometimes different results in the same person on different occasions. Of all the techniques tested for this book, those involving the perineum were most likely to cause confusion, consternation, or simply get little response. On the other hand, testers report, when they work for you, they really do work.

- *THE PERINEUM ORGASM.* Again, excite your partner to the point of orgasm by a combination of oral and manual stimulation. Then apply the tip of your tongue to the midpoint of the perineum. Flick rapidly back and forth. Pause. Suck. Flick the tongue rapidly back and forth again. The resulting orgasm will send powerful vibrations throughout the body.

  This failed for both me and my lover, who said he sometimes feels his orgasms throughout his whole body anyway "without the games," depending on how long he is aroused before orgasm and how emotionally connected he feels to his partner at the time. Another couple who tried the technique reported it did work for him, but not for her. He experienced an orgasm that he felt "more throughout" his body than usual. She said, "It delayed my orgasm so long that I finally couldn't come and was irritable the rest of the night." But a third couple had "limited success" for both partners. "I am not sure if we had complete whole-body orgasms, but we definitely felt spasms in other parts of our bodies. For me, the thighs, legs, belly. For him, the orgasm seemed to move up his trunk into his chest."

Chapter Sixteen

ELECTRIC SEX

I love these Fuckerware parties," Marsha said, and everyone laughed at the comparison between "fantasy toys" and Tupperware, both available in the traditional party sales format in a neighborhood near yours. She was holding a small white appliance that looked like an automatic mixer in one hand. "Is this what I think it is?" she asked.

Yes, it was. A Sunbeam coil vibrator, made by the same company that produces mixers, featuring two speeds and an easy-to-grasp handle. Vicki, the saleswoman, or "party coordinator," took it out of Marsha's hand, flipped a switch, held it up in the air. Buzz. Whirr. Giggle. The sounds of a sex toy party, this one in suburban St. Louis, but it could have been in any suburb in America.

Vicki, a community college teacher, made more than $12,000 in commissions last year selling vibrators, lubricants, anal toys, dildoes, lingerie, Velcro handcuffs, vibrating sleeves and cock rings, and other toys, including the "Slapper," a petite leather paddle advertised as "more bark than bite."

"Raise your hand if you've ever made love in a swimming pool?" Vicki asked. Four hands went up. "Well, Joy Jell provides great lubrication for fun in the water. It's similar to your own secretions but it doesn't thin out in the chlorine pool. And you can use it in the bedroom, too, for those nights when you're not quite as wet as you'd like to be."

Joy Jell and a package of batteries were the hostess gifts that night.

"The vibrators and the lingerie are the biggest sellers," Vicki said, as the women passed the merchandise, the snacks, and the one-liners around the circle.

And that night she did sell five vibrators. Not bad for a party of twelve.

"I've got a wand vibrator," Marsha said, writing out her check for thirty dollars for the coil vibrator. "But a girl can always use another one."

If you've ever been to a sex toy party or shopped at an erotic boutique, you know there are many sex toys and aids for playful and adventurous lovers. Few require detailed instructions for use. My favorite is honey dust, sold in an attractive tin, like loose tea, with a brush, much like the one I use for face powder. You dust it on your lover's body and lick it off.

Sex toys were popular in Japan thousands of years ago. Early sex manuals illustrate a bewildering array of devices for use in masturbation and lovemaking. The classic ben-wa balls were introduced in that country. Lonely geishas and courtesans were expected to use them for entertaining themselves when their wealthy clients and lovers were not around. (Wives had no such recourse.) The balls, inserted into the vagina, generated little waves of pleasure as the women rocked in a chair or swing.

Vibrators are, of course, in a class by themselves. They can be used to accelerate arousal and induce orgasm. We can't look to the ancient texts for advice on how to use them. Nor can we get that kind of help in most mainstream sex manuals. Considering the popularity of the devices, it's surprising that so little useful information about them can be found in print.

Shortly after the turn of the century, small battery-operated vibrators were available to doctors to prescribe for their female patients suffering from "hysteria." (Genital massage was the standard treatment for female hysteria among enlightened doctors. The objective was to induce "hysterical paroxysm," or orgasm, which presumably cured the sufferer . . . until she was horny again.) By the 1920s, vibrators were marketed as "massagers" to the general public. Beginning in the 1960s—after female hysteria had been debunked by the American Medical Association—people were told vibrators could help women who were rarely or never orgasmic to reach orgasm during intercourse—and also warned they might be "addictive." Can you really get so attached to an electric climax that you can't come any other way? Not likely, the experts say.

Both men and women enjoy the wide range of sexual stimulation provided by vibrators during masturbation. They can also enhance partner sex. Vibrators come in many shapes and sizes, including those huge objects that look like King Kong's penis and shouldn't be inserted unless you are King Kong's true mate. They differ from dildoes, also penis-shaped and often oversized, in that they vibrate. Dildoes have no power source and must be wielded by you or a partner.

Some vibrators are attached to plug-in cords and run on the standard 110 volts. Most are battery operated. You may find the best products marketed by the same manufacturers as personal massagers and sold in the small appliances section of department, drug, and discount stores—or next to the blow dryers in the beauty supply shop. They typically have sets of attachments, including one designed to massage the G spot.

"Every woman should have a vibrator in the house," a woman said. "It doesn't matter if you are single or married. There are those times when only the steady comforting hum of a vibrator will take you where you want to go. When I'm tired and stressed, the vibrator is what I want."

"I can't believe I waited so long," said a thirty-eight-year-old woman who bought her first vibrator on a trip to Japan. Also available in this country through the Good Vibrations catalog, the Pink Pearl vibrator, shaped like a bullet, runs on two AA batteries and is meant to be inserted. "I had to read the directions to figure out you put it in like a tampon. Once I got it in there, I knew what to do. Writhe in ecstasy. What a trip!"

The Basic Female Masturbation Technique

• Most women reach orgasm with the vibrator by pressing it against the clitoris, not through vaginal insertion. Experiment by varying the pressure and speed as you move the vibrator around your genitals. If the vibration is too intense even at low speed for direct clitoral contact, move it to the side. Play with prolonging the excitation phase by moving the vibrator back and forth. Tease yourself to a stronger orgasm.

Many women have told me in interviews over the years that they can always have an orgasm using a vibrator even if other forms of masturbation and lovemaking sometimes fail them. Some worry they will become "hooked" on the vibrator and unable to reach orgasm any other way, a fear sex therapists say is largely ungrounded. One woman said, "I can have vibrator orgasms easily, but prefer not to do so. The vibrator is fun for arousal during masturbation, but I like to feel the orgasm in the tips of my fingers. I turn it off when I'm ready to come."

The Basic Male Masturbation Technique

• Start on low speed. Run the vibrator along the shaft, then press it against the base, the scrotum, and the perineum. Experiment with higher speeds and firmer pressures. You can have a stronger climax by resisting the urge to grasp your penis and perform manual masturbation. Used correctly, the vibrator takes longer.

A man who had not used a vibrator on himself until he was in his forties said, "I never teased myself, or played, during masturbation before my girlfriend gave me a vibrator for Valentine's Day. Masturbation was goal oriented for me. I think this little gadget has made me a better lover. I can gauge better when I'm near ejaculation during intercourse and pull back."

COUPLE-PLAY WITH VIBRATORS

- Take turns massaging each other with the vibrator. Move down the body to the genitals, move away, and back again using the vibrator to tease as you would use your mouth or hands.

- Use the vibrator to vary stimulation while caressing your partner's genitals. A woman can hold a vibrator against the back of her hand that is cupping her partner's scrotum or holding his penis. A man can hold the vibrator against the back of his hand as he strokes her labia and the sides of her clitoris.

- Stimulate his (or her) perineum with the vibrator during oral or manual lovemaking.

- Use the G spot attachment to stimulate her vagina during cunnilingus.

- An anal vibrator can be used on the man while the woman performs fellatio or fondles his genitals, or on the woman while the man performs cunnilingus or fondles her genitals. Select a modest size and start with a low speed. Use lubrication and proceed with caution.

The sensations produced by an anal vibrator are incredibly exciting. One man said, "The first time my wife used the anal vibrator on me, I ejaculated on my chin. You don't

shoot that far at my age—forty-five—under most circumstances."

- Insert a wand-shaped vibrator between your bodies during intercourse. He will feel indirect vibrations throughout
his penis inside her vagina while she gets clitoral stimulation.

$\mathscr{S}$EXATIONAL SECRETS

This book is meant to help you improve technique while nurturing your sense of play and encouraging your passion. I hope you
will continue to use it the same way you would a gourmet cook-
book. Pick a "recipe" and try it. If you like the result, try it again. If
you don't, flip through the pages and find something else. Sexational
lovemaking is meant to be a pleasurable pastime, not a challenge.
And as much as I have dwelled on technique, I don't want you to
think that technique is *all*.

Michel, the international gigolo, told me, "Women are drawn
to my vulnerability, my ability to listen, my need of them on many
levels. If they were not drawn, they would never know how good I
am in bed."

And Monique, the French courtesan, said, "Men pay for everything we are, not merely our skills in bed."

In other words, a good lover, even one who is paid, combines
skill with many other qualities. It seems fitting to close with a quo-
tation from Anaïs Nin, the erotic diarist whose life and work celebrated passion:

"Sex loses all its power and magic when it becomes explicit,
mechanical, overdone, when it becomes a mechanistic obsession. It
is wrong not to mix sex with emotion, hunger, desire, lust, whims,
caprices, personal ties, deeper relationships that change its color, fla-
vor, rhythms. . . ."

Sexation springs forth from this heady mix.